Twayne's English Authors Series

Thomas Carew

TEAS 214

THOMAS CAREW

By LYNN SADLER

Bennett College

TWAYNE PUBLISHERS

A DIVISION OF G. K. HALL & CO., BOSTON

Copyright © 1979 by G. K. Hall & Co.

Published in 1979 by Twayne Publishers,
A Division of G. K. Hall & Co.
All Rights Reserved

Printed on permanent/durable acid-free paper and bound
in the United States of America

First Printing

Library of Congress Cataloging in Publication Data

Sadler, Lynn.
Thomas Carew.

(Twayne's English authors series : TEAS 214)
Bibliography: p. 161 - 64
Includes index.
1.   Carew, Thomas, 1595? - 1639?—Criticism and
interpretation.
PR3339.C2Z79   821'.4   78-18796
ISBN 0-8057-6683-9

Contents

About the Author

Mary Lynn Veach Sadler was graduated from Duke University (B.A.) and the University of Illinois (M.A., Ph.D.). She has held a postdoctoral research grant from the Clark Library and UCLA for work on Milton.

She has taught at Agnes Scott College, Drake University, and North Carolina Agricultural and Technical State University. Currently, she is Chairperson of the Department of Communications and Director of the Division of Humanities at Bennett College. She received an award for "Extraordinary Undergraduate Teaching" from Drake University.

Dr. Sadler has published widely on Milton. Her other publications include articles on Chaucer, Shakespeare, Greene, Lovelace, Donne, Ellison, and alchemy. She has also written the Twayne volume on John Bunyan.

Having recently turned to creative writing, she has written a novella and four novels.

Preface

Because of his derivativeness as a poet, Thomas Carew has been studied principally for his relations to Elizabethan, Baroque, Cavalier, Donnean-Metaphysical, and Jonsonian-Classical poetry. Much of the criticism of Carew to date has confined itself to his sources. The tendency has been to conclude that an image in a Carew poem may be well drawn but that Donne could have drawn it far better or that a Carew verse may be smooth but that Jonson could have made it smoother.

Carew has also had the misfortune to be known mainly as an anthology poet. His contemporary reputation of libertine has persisted into our period, for the poems anthologized are inevitably some of the amorous, erotic lyrics.

The one other work of Carew that is widely known is his elegy on John Donne. While this poem is universally admired, its critics too frequently simply point to it to suggest what Carew could have accomplished had he been more serious as a poet or to suggest the catalytic power of Donne's influence.

The result is that Carew is mainly known as a facile versifier of erotic love poems who happened to write an extraordinary elegy on Donne. The paradox of that assessment demands exploration, but only a few modern critics have given more than passing attention to Carew and certainly not to this curious paradox about him. Charles Sembower ("A Note on the Verse Structure of Carew") first brought notice to the preciseness of his prosody. The view of Carew as a poetic craftsman has been extended by Rufus Blanshard ("Thomas Carew's Master Figures"). More recently, D. F. Rauber ("Carew Redivivus") has presented Carew as the most intellectual poet of his period. The one book-length study, by Edward I. Selig, has ably established Carew's individuality and has provided an organization of his work as a whole. It is selective of the poems analyzed, however, and does not deal with Carew's masque, *Coelum Britannicum*.

Before the student can decide whether the more recent view of Carew—that he is a craftsman and a poet in his own right—is apt, he or she must be aware of what Carew wrote. The main purpose of this book is to provide at least a limited introduction to the entire canon of Thomas Carew. The primary focus is on the works themselves, not on the influences on them (though these are generally noted in passing, and care is taken to provide direction for their further study). Paraphrase of the works has been employed perforce, but attempts are made to emphasize impressive successes (and failures) in both content and prosody.

A new organization of Carew's canon is presented here. Approximately three-fourths of his works are love poems. They are studied in two chapters: one concentrates on the poems he wrote for his adored and pseudonymous "Celia"; the other discusses the poems addressed to his "mistress" (probably also Celia) and the more anonymous group rounding out his lyrical vein. Another chapter claims a seriousness usually denied Carew as it explores his comments on poetry and the poet even within the love lyrics. It then goes on to his critical treatments of Donne, Jonson, and others. The remainder of Carew's output is considered in chapters on occasional verses and on *Coelum Britannicum*. A short last chapter summarizes Carew's critical reputation and attempts to locate his "place" in literary history.

A special indebtedness must be acknowledged to the editor of the standard edition of Carew's works, Professor Rhodes Dunlap, especially for his illumination of Carew's sources, and to Oxford University Press for permission to use this edition.

In certain instances, the italics, *u/v*, *i/j*, and periods after the titles of poems, in the standard edition, have been regularized to conform with modern usage.

Chronology

"Conquest by flight" published.

1639/40   Carew dies, on or about March 21.
1640   First edition of Carew's *Poems*, by Thomas Walkley.
1642   Walkley's second edition of the *Poems*.
1651   Third edition of the *Poems* by Humphrey Moseley.
1670   Fourth edition of the *Poems* by Henry Herringman.

CHAPTER 1

Carew's Life and "School" of Poetry

A S one can see from the Chronology, facts about the life of Thomas Carew are rare. The would-be biographer is further hampered by the confusion and ambiguities that lace such "facts" as do exist. Was he born in 1594 or 1595? Where was he born? Which of the three contemporaries, Thomas Carew / Carey, is the poet? Was his college Merton or Corpus Christi? Did he die in 1638 or 1639 at age forty-four, in 1640 at age forty-five, in 1645 at age fifty, or when he was much older? Did he die of syphilis? Did he receive the Manor of Sunninghill from King James or King Charles, and was it recalled for lack of payment before or at his death? Did he marry a rich widow? Did he marry at all? Did he become Ben Jonson's "research assistant" for a history of Henry V? Which is his authentic portrait? Is there a portrait of Carew? The problems indicated here persist into *current* criticism, not to mention the disorder among older treatments of Carew.

Only ten poems were published during Carew's life, and some of those lacked his name and his authorization. His masque, *Coelum Britannicum,* was also published without his name. His signature in the Oxford subscription register and three letters survive. For the remainder of his works and life story, modern critics have been obliged to seek manuscripts, random records, anthologies, and miscellanies. Even the advent of the standard edition in 1949 has not entirely settled the inconsistencies among this mishmash of materials.

I   *Generally Accepted Information about Carew*

Thomas Carew was born, perhaps in the family county of Kent, though he is not listed in its baptismal records, in 1594 or 1595. His clan was well connected; and his father, Matthew, hailed by one critic as his "son's worst enemy,"[1] was a Master in Chancery. He eventually practiced law in London and was knighted about 1603. Sir Matthew would have liked for his son to become a lawyer, too.

The family, according to its antiquarian, Richard Carew, Thomas's cousin, "came over" with William the Conqueror and took its name from *carru*, "plow." However, Professor Rhodes Dunlap derives the surname from Carew (Caer Yw) Castle, County Carmarthen.[2] Whatever its etymology, its pronunciation is also in doubt: "Ca-*rew*" versus "*Car*-ey." The latter seems the more promising[3] and perhaps accounts for at least part of the confusion of Thomas Carew, the poet, with the two contemporaries who spelled their names "Thomas Carey."

The first Thomas Carey (1597 - 1634), the son of the Earl of Monmouth, was a favorite of James I and served as Groom of the Bed-Chamber to the King. He married one Margaret Smith, received Sunninghill Manor from King James, and died on April 9, 1634. To make matters more confusing, he, like Thomas Carew, the poet under discussion, had poems (two) set to music by Henry Lawes. The second Thomas Carey was a member of Gray's Inn and Gentleman-Porter of the Tower. He translated Puget de la Serre's *Mirrour which flatters not*.

While the information about his early education is also scant, it is known that Carew entered Merton College, Oxford, in June 1608, at age thirteen. He received his B.A. on January 31, 1610 / 11, somewhat early, and, by February, was a reader in the Bodleian Library, being incorporated a B.A. of Cambridge in 1612. He was apparently meant to follow his father in the pursuit of law and was admitted to the Middle Temple on August 6, 1612. The events forestalling his projected legal career remain undetermined.

II   *Carew and the Carletons*

Perhaps the financial reverses that plagued Sir Matthew Carew during his last years brought about Thomas's change of mind about the profession of lawyer. At any rate—no doubt with the urging of his father, who recorded that his son "studied the law very little"—he entered the service of Sir Dudley Carleton, probably in the position of secretary. Lady Carleton was Sir Matthew Carew's niece. Thus Thomas was exposed to the culture of Italy, where Carleton was ambassador to Venice in 1613. Italian influence is marked in his poetry, and a letter by him, dated 1616, speaks of the languages he was able to acquire in Carleton's service. He remained in this position during Sir Dudley's embassy to The Hague. Sometime, however, in the course of this second tour of duty, a disruption in relations occurred. Carleton somehow discovered Carew's written slanders ("to set his head aworke without any meaneng either to shew it to anye, or to make any other use therof then to hym selfe"[4]) of Lady Carleton and himself. Carew was not told of the discovery; rather, Lord Carleton urged his return to England to find other employment that would more readily advance his career.

Once back home, about the middle of August 1616, Thomas acted upon Sir Dudley's advice. He first approached, unsuccessfully, his kinsman Lord Carew, who had recently become a member of the Privy Council. Next he turned to Thomas Howard, the Earl of Arundel, whom he had apparently met in Italy and who favored Thomas's suit but had already promised the place being sought to another. While engaged in this search for a position, Thomas plied Lord Carleton with letters citing his failures to secure other employment and requested that he be allowed to return to his "primum mobile,"[5] the director of his course. He also begged for a letter of recommendation to the Earl of Arundel. His father, too, baffled by his son's unannounced arrival in England, wrote to his kinsman in letters proclaiming his dismay at the turn of Thomas's fortunes. Sir Matthew's own financial troubles were deepening, and the loan which Carleton had promised to help him meet the mortgage on his London home was not forthcoming. Ultimately, Lord Carleton had his agent, Edward Sherburne, inform the old man (and the Earl of Arundel) of the reasons for Thomas's dismissal. In Sherburne's presence, Sir Matthew called his unrepentant son to account, thereby launching the quarrel that persisted between them.

Thomas seems to have spent this difficult period (1616 - 18) in visiting those whose connections might help him, in cutting a fine figure, and in continuing his tendency to make ill-chosen comments. He accompanied his brother Matthew to Woodstock, where the court was. He certainly saw Lady Carleton's stepfather, Sir Henry Savile, a kinsman by marriage and Warden of Merton College during Thomas's tenure there. He proceeded to incense his onetime benefactor further with Savile's subsequent report that Thomas had spoken lightly of Sir Dudley Carleton's horses. Carew was obviously not very tactful; but whether, as his father indicated by letter to Sir Dudley (September 1, 1616), he "thought too highly of himself" and suffered from "self-pride," cannot be surely known.

His demand for a letter of apology to Carleton being of no avail, the ailing father gave his son up for lost and complained bitterly of him in a letter to Carleton dated October 4, 1617. Sir Matthew recorded, not without some sense of God's justice, that Thomas now suffered from the "new disease" (presumably syphilis)[6] and that all of his plans for his son had come to naught. Sir Matthew died on August 2, 1618, at age eighty-five. Of his three children, he was pleased only with his daughter.

III   Duties in France and England

Perhaps as a result of some of his visiting patterns during the period of his rift with Carleton and his father, Carew was making his way at court. He is recorded as being among the most elegant in attendance when Charles was installed as Prince of Wales on November 4, 1616. He may also have begun his wooing of the lady celebrated in so many of his poems as "Celia." Finally, in May of 1619, he accompanied Sir Edward Herbert (later Lord Herbert of Cherbury, also a poet) in his embassy to Paris and became the fast friend of John Crofts, whose family home of Saxham was to assume an important place in his life and poetry. A number of his poems seem to have been written during his stay in France. He may also have met, in Paris, the Italian, Giambattista Marino, who influenced his poetic style.

Much later, during the period from 1630 - 33, he cemented his ties with the English court, being named, first, Gentleman of the Privy Chamber Extraordinary and then Sewer in Ordinary to the King.[7] The latter appointment was made despite the fact that the Scots were promoting another candidate. A life of some ease was thus achieved, and Carew became known as one of the wittiest poets and courtiers of Charles I.

IV   Anecdotes about Carew

Carew's contemporary reputation as a witty courtier is borne out by a series of anecdotes told of him. For example, George Clarke, once Lord of the Admiralty, reported to Sir John Percival this confirmation of Carew's "quickness." Lighting King Charles to Henrietta Maria's chamber, Carew saw Jermyn Lord St. Albans with his arm around the Queen's neck. He feigned a stumble, put out the light, and thus helped to secure the gentleman's escape.

While the King never knew of the episode, the Queen naturally became one of Carew's great patrons.

In the winter of 1624 - 25, Carew was rumored to be on the verge of marrying the rich widow of Sir George Smith. His friend, fellow poet, and fellow Gentleman of the Privy Chamber, Sir John Suckling, chided him for such a rash proposal and received Carew's clever reply. Both letters were printed in parallel columns, paragraph for paragraph, with Carew forcefully surmounting each charge (e.g., ". . . . I'le marry a *Widow*, who is rather the *chewer*, then *thing chewed*"[8]). So far as is known, Carew was never married.

One report, in a letter from James Howell to Sir Thomas Hawke on April 5, 1636, provides a glimpse of Carew the man: "I was invited yesternight to a solemn supper by B. J. [Ben Jonson], where you were deeply remembered; there was good company, excellent cheer, choice wines, and jovial welcome: one thing intervened, which almost spoiled the relish of the rest, that B. began to engross all the discourse, to vapour extremely of himself and by vilifying others to magnify his own muse. T. Ca. [Thomas Carew] buzzed me in the ear, that though Ben had barrelled up a great deal of knowledge, yet it seems he had not read the *Ethics,* which, among other Precepts of Morality, forbid Self-commendation."[9] As will be seen, Carew was no submissive "Son of Ben," but could see faults wherever they were to be found.

Finally, there is the story of the supposed deathbed recantation, though variations of this anecdote are so characteristically applied to famous men as to be immediately suspect. Like many of his peers at Charles I's court, Carew was reputed to be a profligate and a libertine. During one of his illnesses (another bout of syphilis?), when he thought he was dying, he sent for John Hales, who had been a fellow of Merton College in 1606, and who had become connected with Thomas by marriage. At the poet's promise to amend his life, Hales gave him absolution. However, upon recovering, Carew resumed his "life scandalous." Then, according to information gathered by Izaak Walton for a life of Hales, in the poet's last illness when he again called upon Hales for spiritual aid, he was refused both the sacrament and absolution. The account of this double repentance is also provided by Joseph Hunter in the *Chorus Vatum Anglicanorum* from the narration of Lady Salter, to whose son Hales was tutor.

The truth of this tale of contrition cannot be known, but Carew had a reputation for licentiousness such that his poems were blasted in Parliament as part of the traffic of pornography afoot in London. And Lord Clarendon, Carew's friend, records (thereby adding more confusion as to the length of Thomas's life): ". . . his Glory was that after fifty Years of his Life, spent with less Severity or Exactness than it ought to have been, He died with the greatest Remorse for that Licence, and with the greatest Manifestation of Christianity, that his best Friends could desire." [10]

Others cite Carew's choice of Psalms for translation and adaptation, as well as his self-"laceration" in "To My worthy friend Master Geo. Sand[y]s, on his translation of the Psalmes," as evidence of his intended correction of his life. The Psalms he paraphrased, however, were probably early efforts written during his first siege of syphilis while he was under his father's care. They show no particular personal revelations. Of the nine Psalms he elected to deal with, only Numbers 51 and 119 have any special penitential cast. The commendation of Sandys[11] seems little more than the homage of one poet to another upon such an occasion:

> I Presse not to the Quire, nor dare I greet
> The holy place with my unhallowed feet;
> My unwasht Muse, polutes not things Divine,
> Nor mingles her prophaner notes with thine;
> Here, humbly at the porch she listning stayes,
> And with glad eares sucks in thy sacred layes.

> Perhaps my restlesse soule, tyr'de with persuit
> Of mortall beauty, seeking without fruit
> Contentment there, which hath not, when enjoy'd,
> Quencht all her thirst, nor satisfi'd, though cloy'd;
> Weary of her vaine search below, Above
> In the first Faire may find th' immortall Love.
> (ll. 1 - 6, 23 - 28)[12]

V *The Absence of a Portrait of Carew*

Another bit of gossip introduces the problems concerning the authenticity of the portraits of the poet. Carew's friend Thomas Killigrew quarreled with Cecilia Crofts (later his wife) and asked Carew to intervene. To oblige, Carew wrote the poem "Jealousie," used in a masque at Whitehall Palace in 1633 and included in Killigrew's play, *Cicilia and Clorinda, or Love in Arms* (written 1649 - 50). Horace Walpole subsequently reported, quoting other sources, that Anthony Van Dyck's 1638 portrait of Killigrew and

Carew commemorated this argument of the lovers and Carew's service as intermediary. However, Professor Dunlap has conclusively shown that this is an impossible interpretation of the origin of the portrait.[13]

Van Dyke's painting, in the Royal Collection of Windsor Castle, shows Killigrew on the left holding a paper with two female figures drawn on pedestals. On the right, Carew holds a paper, too. Following the lead of Ernest Law's study of the Van Dyck pictures at Windsor, Dunlap suggests that the two women were intended for a sepulchral monument to Cecilia Crofts Killigrew and to the Countess of Cleveland, who died in 1637 / 38; both were sisters of John Crofts. Carew's paper may represent his avocation of poet. While Law has discounted the authenticity of the likeness of Carew, Professor Dunlap accepts this half of the Van Dyck portrait as the only genuine one of the poet. However, since the standard edition of Carew's works was published, further research has been done on the Van Dyck portrait. The figure once thought to be Carew is almost certainly Thomas Killigrew's brother-in-law, William, Lord Crofts.[14]

Many of Carew's editors and critics, including one publishing as recently as 1960, have used for Carew's picture one from a medal produced by Jean Warin / Varin of Thomas Carey, the Gentleman of the Bedchamber. William Carew Hazlitt went so far as to alter the medal's inscription in order to use a copy of it for his edition of Carew in 1870.

VI *Carew's Death*

Carew's "To my friend G. N. [Gilbert North?] from Wrest" (86 - 89), probably his last poem, sheds some light on the actual facts of his death. It contrasts the munificence of Wrest Park Manor in Bedfordshire, which belonged to the De Greys, with the deprivation of the expedition led by King Charles against Scotland in 1639:

> I Breathe (sweet *Ghib:*) the temperate ayre of *Wrest*
> Where I no more with raging stormes opprest,
> Weare the cold nights out by the bankes of Tweed,
> On the bleake Mountains, where fierce tempests breed,
> And everlasting Winter dwells; where milde
> *Favonius*, and the Vernall windes exilde,
> Did never spread their wings: but the wilde North
> Brings sterill Fearne, Thistles, and Brambles forth.
>   (ll. 1 - 8)

Carew apparently was with Charles in this First Bishops' War, and
the rigors they encountered, it is conjectured, hastened his death,
which occurred about March 21, 1639 / 40. At any rate, after a
rather costly funeral, he was buried in St. Anne's Chapel, the
Church of St. Dunstan's-in-the-West. The church was remodeled in
the early nineteenth century, and no trace of the tomb of Thomas
Carew is now to be found.

Despite their estrangement, Thomas was interred beside Sir
Matthew Carew, a fact all the more unexpected in view of the distance between Thomas and the rest of the family. After Matthew
Carew's death, his London house was sold, and his widow went to
live with her older son, Matthew, in the country. Her highly de-
tailed will, dispensing properties and goods down to her
grandchildren, servants, and tenants, failed to mention Thomas. It
seems likely that no reconciliation was ever effected.

VII   Carew's "School" of Poetry

Thomas Carew continues to be presented principally in
anthologies, which label him, without very careful qualification, a
"Cavalier" poet along with Sir John Suckling and Richard
Lovelace. The tag derives from their association with King Charles,
from their use of military imagery, and particularly from their supposed lack of high seriousness. The two greatest influences upon his
poetry are John Donne[15] and Ben Jonson.[16] He owes much directly
to the Classical tradition: specifically to the Latin poets, as Ovid
(Publius Ovidius Naso), Gaius Valerius Catullus, and Sextus Propertius;[17] and more generally to the Greeks, as Anacreon and other
lyric poets and the *Greek Anthology*. Constant echoes of the
Elizabethan "Petrarchan"[18] sonneteers are also to be found in
Carew's poems. Strongly marked are the effects of the Continental
poets: from France, Pontus de Tyard, Pierre de Ronsard, Philippe
Desportes, and the whole *libertin* (libertine) tradition;[19] from Italy,
Torquato Tasso, Giovanni Battista Guarini, and especially the great
leader of the Baroque, Giambattista Marino, whom Carew probably
met in Paris.[20]

Carew assimilates all of these forces and influences and yet
stamps his poetry with his own witty mark. As a lyricist and a court
poet, mildly cynical and skeptical, he combines the accents of pure
worship of the lady from the Petrarchan tradition with a prosaic,
rather detached, worldliness. Commendatory and occasional verse

fill most of his pages; but he is best known as a writer of amorous, not infrequently erotic, poetry. Typically, he polishes his gemlike poems with care, revising and improving.[21] He may nonetheless occasionally lapse into inexact syntax, not so excessively, however, as his fellow Cavalier, Richard Lovelace. If Sir John Suckling's description in "A Sessions of the Poets" (c. 1638) can be taken as any indication, Carew seems to have had a reputation among his contemporaries similar to that of his mentor, Ben Jonson—his Muse was "hard-bound," delivering her offspring only with hard work and concentration. Carew learned this craftsmanship from Jonson[22] and his attitude toward it from the Elizabethans; for, generally, the reader is hardly aware of effort in his poems. He has imbibed the *sprezzatura* tradition of Edmund Spenser and Sir Philip Sidney and so hides his labor under a smooth demeanor that earned him the dubious later reputation of writing effortlessly and sometimes carelessly.

This reputation for lack of care was aided by the slender content of the majority of his poems. The court poetry of his day did not moralize or philosophize. Writing poetry was still an avocation of the courtier, who used it to demonstrate his own and the court's urbanity. The reader must accept that view of poetry before accusing Carew of a failure of depth and high purpose as a poet.

Carew does avoid the large-scale allegories of the Elizabethans but occasionally adopts such Petrarchan analogies as the "ship of love" or the "besieged fort." Similarly, he may fleetingly dip into Neo-Platonic lore but could never be labeled a "Neo-Platonist" in the manner of Spenser. At the same time, he borrows from Italian and French poets who were interested in both Petrarchanism and Neo-Platonism.[23]

From Donne (and his own short-lived legal training), he derives his use of logic; his conversational, often colloquial tone in the midst of the most "hallowed" service at his lady's shrine; perhaps his occasional obscurity; some of his conceits, especially those he uses to show their limitations and obsolescence; much of his wit; and his use of well-developed, emphatic, and bold metaphors and occasional juxtapositions of disparate materials. In contrast to the poetry of Donne, Carew's poetry remains almost totally secular, with no flights of mysticism. He is also more conscious of regularity of meter than is Donne, to the extent that Pope ultimately included him in the School of Waller and that modern critics find in his works a tone of civility and a precision of form (both from Jonson and the Classical writers) that anticipated Pope and other Neoclassical and Augustan poets.

Perhaps an examination of two poems, the second better than the first, will help to point out the difficulties of classifying Carew even at his least original.

The first, "To her in absence. A Ship" (23), is thoroughly derivative:

> Tost in a troubled sea of griefes, I floate
> Farre from the shore, in a storme-beaten boat,
> Where my sad thoughts doe (like the compasse) show
> The severall points from which crosse winds doe blow.
> My heart doth like the needle toucht with love 5
> Still fixt on you, point which way I would move.
> You are the bright Pole-starre, which in the darke
> Of this long absence, guides my wandring barke.
> Love is the Pilot, but o're-come with feare
> Of your displeasure, dares not homewards steare; 10
> My fearefull hope hangs on my trembling sayle;
> Nothing is wanting but a gentle gale,
> Which pleasant breath must blow from your sweet lip:
> Bid it but move, and quick as thought this Ship
> Into your armes, which are my port, will flye 15
> Where it for ever shall at Anchor lye.

Among its most positive attributes, aside from the smooth, pentameter couplets, is the concentration upon developing the Petrarchan conceit of the unrequited lover adrift on a "sea of griefes" (also adumbrated by Classical writers like Catullus and Virgil). Though a different kind of compass, the compass image may suggest Donne as well as Carew's own "An Excuse of absence" (131) and "To *Celia*, upon Love's Ubiquity" (123 - 24); but it remains Elizabethan here rather than Metaphysical or Donnean. This claim is further supported by the fact that the companion image ("You are the bright Pole-starre") evokes comparison with Shakespeare's Sonnet 116, ll. 5 - 8.[24] Carew's poem, however, achieves a simplicity of statement that makes the reader entirely forget the combined influences. Sounded at the last is a hope of amendment that sets itself in opposition to the "head-banging," forlorn lover of sonnet lore. The natural, instinctive sweetness in the lady herself belies the "disdainful one" of the same school.

The second poem, "The Comparison" (98 - 99), proves that Carew knows the ways of Elizabethan compliment and commendation, yet immediately indicates that he is going to adopt the skeptical tone of Shakespeare's or Donne's deflation of Petrarchan conceits (e.g., Sonnet 130 or "The Canonization," respectively):

> Dearest thy tresses are not threads of gold,
> Thy eyes of Diamonds, nor doe I hold
> Thy lips for Rubies: Thy fair cheekes to be
> Fresh Roses; or thy teeth of Ivorie:
> Thy skin that doth thy daintie bodie sheath   5
> Not Alablaster [*sic*] is, nor dost thou breath
> *Arabian* odours, those the earth brings forth
> Compar'd with which would but impaire thy worth.
> Such may be others Mistresses, but mine
> Holds nothing earthly, but is all divine.   10
> Thy tresses are those rayes that doe arise
> Not from one Sunne, but two; Such are thy eyes:
> Thy lips congealed Nectar are, and such
> As but a Deitie, there's none dare touch.
> The perfect crimson that thy cheeke doth cloath   15
> (But onely that it farre exceeds them both)
> *Aurora's* blush resembles, or that redd
> That *Iris* struts in when her mantl's spred.
> Thy teeth in white doe *Leda's* Swan exceede,
> Thy skin's a heavenly and immortall weede,   20
> And when thou breath'st, the winds are readie strait
> To filch it from thee, and doe therefore wait
> Close at thy lips, and snatching it from thence
> Beare it to Heaven, where 'tis *Joves* frankincense.
> Faire Goddesse, since thy feature makes thee one,   25
> Yet be not such for these respects alone;
> But as you are divine in outward view
> So be within as faire, as good, as true.

Carew is not so crass as Shakespeare, avoiding such excesses as "in some perfumes is there more delight / Than in the breath that from my mistress reeks." Yet he takes the Shakespearean route of rebuking the inanities of the traditional Petrarchan and Elizabethan blazon (ll. 1 - 8). Then he shocks the reader by dropping the realism of Shakespeare's final compliment to trumpet forth extravagances more extravagant than those he has rejected (ll. 9 - 24). These lines also, however, employ a characteristic Carew touch of logic, as they build to the obvious conclusion. Since the poet's mistress lacks the attributes of mortal mistresses, he can only accept that she is divine. Having drawn parallel after parallel with Classical figures, the poet must address her in the new identity he has provided for her: "Faire Goddesse, since thy feature makes thee one."

Then comes an additional witty twist, strangely reinstating at least part of the Petrarchan tradition he has banished—the emphasis on spiritual as well as physical beauty. Yet this reinstatement is tempered by realism and stated as directly, gracefully, and simply as are the last lines of "To her in absence. A Ship." (Carew is almost without exception excellent in his endings.) The final couplet is worth repeating: "But as you are divine in outward view / So be within as faire, as good, as true." Many women can look like goddesses. The trick is to be better-than-mortal internally. Neither does there seem to be any shrinking of the meaning of these lines to the libertine view that "being 'good' means being my mistress."

Carew is neither totally Jonsonian, Donnean, Elizabethan, nor Cavalier. When he is at his best, synergism occurs.

The two poems above are in Carew's favorite form, iambic pentameter couplets. The striving for regularity is emphasized by the use of elision or telescoping of syllables (as l. 4 of "To her in absence. A Ship" and ll. 7, 20, and 24 of "The Comparison").

The regularity one so often finds in Carew's poetry has been partially responsible for his being known as a facile, largely negligible poet. Yet his verse forms show a great variety and care,[25] and he experiments rather frequently with catalexis or lines terminating in imperfect feet, and with truncation or omission of syllables at the beginning of lines. Some of his best-known poems in fact contain truncated lines (e.g., "Disdaine returned," 18), catalectic lines (e.g., "An Excuse of absence," 131), or both (e.g., "The Complement," 99 - 101). At his most successful, Carew seems aware of form as meaning.

Of the 130 canonical poems, which include nine translations from the Psalms, some eighty employ rhyming couplets. Approximately thirty-eight of those are in pentameter and thirty-seven in tetrameter (octosyllabic couplets). Classical influence shows itself especially in Carew's tetrameter lines (as in "A New-yeares gift. To the King," 89). The tetrameter poems may use various stanzaic patterns and may display shifts to pentameter by catalexis or in the final couplet. For the poems, the iambic foot is Carew's overwhelming choice, with trochaic variations worth noting in "To my Cousin (C.R.) marrying my Lady (A.)" (47) and "The tinder" (104). Both in couplets and in stanza forms, Carew is fond of alternating line length and sometimes uses such combinations as trimeter and dimeter, tetrameter and dimeter, tetrameter and trimeter, or pentameter and dimeter. Several (e.g., "Upon some alterations in my Mistresse, after my departure into France," 24) present pentameter, dimeter, trimeter, and tetrameter lines.

After rhyming couplets, Carew prefers six-line stanzas (used in sixteen poems). Most of these rhyme ababcc, but there are variations. He provides a refrain for one ("Song. To a Lady not yet enjoy'd by her Husband," 36) and occasionally adds an extra couplet to the last stanza or uses a final couplet, set off from the poem, as a coda for the whole.

Couplet stanzas are used in one ("Psalme 119," 144 - 49) of the translations of the Psalms (which, despite being early projects, show much experimentation). The eight poems in tercets are all regular (aaa) except for the unusual handling of the rhyme scheme in "An Hymeneall Song on the Nuptials of the Lady *Ann Wentworth*, and the Lord *Lovelace*" (114). Six poems are in quatrains, ten in five-line stanzas, two in seven-line stanzas, two in eight-line stanzas, and one in eleven-line stanzas. Carew has four "sonnets," so-called only from the fourteen lines in each, for they are highly experimental.

Carew does not always or often in fact succeed in making the form of the verse inherently functional. He is best at creating the illusion that each stanza or unit (often a verse paragraph) moves deftly to the point of the whole poem. His method is frequently the use of graceful, easy caesuras within the line and connective words at the beginning of lines. This illusion of logical movement, culminating in a terse, sometimes gnomic final couplet or statement, is one of his principal characteristics and prevents him from being cloyingly sweet. The sensation of movement also derives from his free-flowing couplets, almost never end-stopped but spilling over to form whole units (as "paragraphs") of thought.

CHAPTER 2

Carew and Celia

Pᴿᴼᴾᴱᴿᵀᴵᵁˢ and Cynthia, Catullus and Lesbia, Petrarch and Laura, Dante and Beatrice, Suckling and Lucasta, Waller and Sacharissa, Habington and Castara—many poets have been renowned for allegiance to a lady celebrated in their poems. And sometime about 1616, Thomas Carew probably began his wooing of the still-unidentified "Celia," a pseudonym popular in Renaissance verse.

Two critics have attempted to synthesize what is known of her; but in making their cases, they have included, in addition to the Celia poems proper, those addressed to or dealing with the more generalized "mistress" of the poet-lover. According to Arthur Vincent,

. . . even if the person so addressed by Carew was always the same, there is little information about her to be gleaned from the poems she inspired. These, however, convey the impression that there was some real person hidden under the name, although they have little to say as to any particular attributes which might lead to her identification. She was not beautiful, if we may trust the judgment of one who, when the poet praised his mistress's beauty, said he was blind . . . , but, if the poet himself may be trusted, she had a soul-stirring voice . . . ; she could weep when her lover left her . . . ; but, when he came back from France, he noticed some alterations . . . ; perhaps she had begun to alter when she commanded the return of her letters . . . , and, to judge from the general tone of what may be taken to be subsequent addresses to her, she was never the same again.[1]

A further note of caution weaves through the "slender story" found by Rhodes Dunlap: ". . . the lady had golden hair, sang divinely, and was at home in noble houses; she returned the poet's love and wept at his departure, perhaps to France in 1619; during his absence she underwent a change of heart and demanded the return of her letters; later she married another, not happily; and after the

24

marriage she was again courted by Carew. But there is no external evidence."[2]

Carew's "To Master W[alter]. Mountague" (78 - 79), though it is not, as the title indicates, about Celia, suggests that her name was indelibly and seriously linked with that of Carew. In iambic pentameter couplets more perfunctory than is usual with him, the poet files a "deposition"[3] against Montagu for leaving his country and his friend:

> . . . but I
> Have a just private quarrell to defie
> And call you Coward, thus to run away
> When you had pierc'd my heart, not daring stay
> Till I redeem'd my honour; but I sweare
> By *Celia's* eyes, by the same force to teare
> Your heart from you, or not to end this strife
> Till I or find revenge, or lose my life.
> (ll. 17 - 24)

While this reference does not conclusively prove that "Celia" represents a real woman, it does suggest that her identity is known to the friend as well as the poet.

Besides "To Master W. Mountague," twenty-three other poems by Carew mention Celia specifically. Although it is impossible to date these Celia poems with certainty, one can construct from them a fairly reasonable series of events from courting to parting. Additionally, they show the poet in love and in a variety of attitudes toward the courtier's graceful game of love.

I *The Courtship of Celia and the Dangers of Time*

In "Loves Courtship" (107 - 108), the poet vows that, if "lovely *Celia*" will but "kisse" and "be kind," they "will make the Gods confesse, / Mortals enjoy some happiness" (ll. 4 - 5). In fact, Mars would make her his "immortall Queene" or become mortal for her sake if he could but behold Celia in the speaker's arms. And Venus would become a merely "Silly Queene" to boast of her *one* Cupid when the poet-lover can see "Ten thousand *Cupids* in thy eye" (l. 15). Moreover, the sun will not be able to behold their bliss, for Celia's eyes will dazzle his. Even so, if she fears that the sun will "betray" her with his light, the lover can "eclipse her from his sight" (l. 20). While he so protects her, he begs that she will gently cry, "*Celia* yields" (l. 23).

Thus far, the poem seems to combine the most traditional kinds of commendation and wooing, punctuated effectively by the short (dimeter), truncated third line enveloped between the two tetrameter couplets in each of its five five-line stanzas.[4] Similarities to Donne (ll. 18 - 20) and to Shakespeare (ll. 6 - 10), as well as the ubiquitous facts that his love gives the gods pause for thought and that her eyes dazzle the sun, demark this poem as totally within old courses. However, the final couplet, sounding itself proverbial, alters the tone from clever adulation to an almost ruthless assertion of the prosaic and too-true:[5] "Maids often loose their Maidenhead, / Ere they set foote in Nuptiall bed."

Inspection in fact convinces the reader that the way to this claim has been carefully prepared both by the logic of the movement and by the metrical form. The figures invoked to prove the argument have been Mars and Venus—involved in one of myth's most famous violations of the sanctity of marriage. By extension, Celia demonstrates her kinship with the gods by yielding up her maidenhead to the poet before her marriage. The understated fact that the poet, too, will be honored by her alignment with gods is also quite characteristic of Carew's subtlety. At the same time, the poem blatantly denies any sweet Elizabethan approach to the gods and goddesses; rather, its use of them brings a tinge of the sardonic Donne to the pursuit of Celia. Still, the potential dissonance of the unrhymed and foreshortened third line of each stanza, suggestive of the sexual demands that are the real issue of the poem, is contained and controlled by the regular couplets surrounding it. Yielding, Celia will be protected by her conformation to the ways of most maids in society. Her performances as goddess and mortal are kept in balance.

Two poems in the Celia group participate in that favored seventeenth-century revival of the Classical *carpe diem* ("seize the day") topos. The first, "Song. Perswasions to enjoy" (16), one of the many poems of Carew set to music by the well-known composer Henry Lawes, declares its motivation in the title. It consists of two six-line stanzas of tetrameter couplets. The second stanza is extended by a final summarizing couplet, the first line of which points back to Stanza 1; the second, to Stanza 2. The first argument is explicitly *carpe diem:* if Celia must decay physically with Time, then, in decidedly harvest images, "let us reape our joyes, / E're time such goodly fruit destroyes" (ll. 5 - 6).

The complexity brought by the second stanza, however, takes the poem beyond the French poet Pierre de Ronsard, accepted as the most obvious influence on Carew here. An alternative to being devoured by Time is being "frozen" in the pastoral world where "that golden fleece must grow / For ever, free from aged snow" (ll. 7 - 8) and where "in vaine" Time beats his wings.[6] Presumably, the implication is that the only conditions under which the second alternative can exist are to be found in the speaker's poetry, which will carry their love to a plateau where love outside of marriage is not a sin. Thus Carew has cleverly restated one of the Elizabethan sonneteers' arguments or "perswasions to enjoy"—to escape time. But the Elizabethans were likely to claim that escape through progeny or through a direct pronouncement of the immortality of verse.

The second *carpe diem* poem is "A Pastorall Dialogue" (42 - 44) between "Celia" and "Cleon," also set to music by Lawes and consisting of fourteen heroic or elegiac quatrians (abab) with alternating tetrameter and trimeter lines. The swain woos Celia to let him wear the "fetters" of her arms and hands. Consenting, she declares their mutual imprisonment, happier for her except that she fears he will break loose again. He swears fidelity beyond beauty's fading, but Celia knows that "Time will destroy them both" (l. 20). Cleon does not, however, dote on her "snow-white skin" but on her "purer mind."[7] Celia's response is that her mind has "lov'd too soone," but Cleon proceeds to prove that "Thou hadst not bin / So faire, if not so kind" (ll. 23 - 24). He bids her make a braid[8] "Of those loose flames, that circle you, / My sunnes, and yet your shade" (ll. 27 - 28) and then makes her admit that her remaining hair must either "change the hue, / Or leave the golden mountaine bare" (ll. 34 - 35). "This small wreathe," contrastingly, will retain "its first native prime" and "The triumphs sing of time" (ll. 38, 40). Admitting the force of his argument, Celia would "cut from thy faire grove, / One branch" (ll. 41 - 42) as another emblem or symbol of their eternal love. Both, Cleon says, are thereby "redeem'd from time"; he, by her grace; she, Celia replies, by his "immortall rime, / Untill the Muses dye" (ll. 47 - 48).

There are unusual features in this pastoral: the sophistication of the shepherd swain's use of logic and argument; the female rather than the male as the wielder of the *carpe diem* topos and its appearance without its usual motivation—a persuasion to love; and the female recognizing her gratitude to poetry and the presence of such a theme *explicitly* within the pastoral. It stands in great contrast to the vision of the pastoral world in the second stanza of "Song. Perswasions to enjoy." Like that poem, however, it finishes on a note different in texture from what has gone before and, in this case, on one that ironically seems to give the lie to their emblems of eternal love:

> Then forth the thicket *Thirsis* rusht,
>   Where he saw all their play:
> The swaine stood still, and smil'd, and blusht,
>   The Nymph fled fast away.

The poet again shies away from the golden vision he has created of two lovers' playful yielding and consonance. The factual, picture-clear opening quatrain gives no warning. Two lovers rest in the shade and thoughtfully discuss their relationship, exploring its philosophical ramifications. Then coolly, abruptly, the reader finds a voyeur, much as Donne's lovers have been spied upon in "The Extasie"; he has seen "all their play" (l. 54). Celia can only flee in shame, for the intruder cannot perceive the philosophizing behind their rapport, just its physical results. The "swain," on the other hand, may smile and blush, but he keeps his place: he knew all along what consummation he built toward. The alliteration of the final quatrain supports the view that this "game of love" has happened many times.

II *Commendations of Celia*

In the manner of the *flyting* or "debate" poem and after the fashion of the Italian poet Giambattista Marino, Celia's "Lips and Eyes" (6) try to force a resolution of the query as to which are more beautiful. A short twelve lines of facile pentameter couplets (with catalexis in ll. 5 - 6, 9 - 10) yield a verbal deadlock, to break which the combatants resort to smiles and tears. Yet the eyes seem to gain a slight advantage,[9] for they, in empathetic response to the shower of "liquid orientall pearle" from Celia's eyes,

> . . . unlockt their pearlie treasure;
> And bad Love judge, whether did adde more grace:
> Weeping or smiling pearles to *Celia's* face.
>   (ll. 10 - 12)

The poem is a light piece, though somewhat of a tour de force, lacking the subtlety of Carew at his best. Unless he uses "golden" images like "liquid orientall pearle" and "pearlie treasure" to mock those images or distance them, he seems sometimes self-conscious in their presence.

The consequences of the beauty of Celia's eyes are also the subject of "A flye that flew into my Mistris her eye" (37 - 38). Subtly playing a variation on the Elizabethan cliché that the mistress's eyes outshine the sun, Carew has the fly, who "us'd to play / In the Sunshine all the day," forswear this arena for "*Celia's* sight," a "new, and unknowne light." It thus becomes the speaker's rival, performs its own (mock-heroic) "blazon" (ll. 9 - 11), and, as a result of this close inspection of Celia's upper perfections (from hand to cheeks and lips), is metamorphosed, in the tradition of Ovid, into a "bird of Paradise." At last, "she" flies into Celia's eyes where, "scorcht in flames, and drown'd in dew," comparable to the "heats" and "colds" of the Petrarchan sonnet lover,[10] the fly, like Phaeton, falls from the "Suns spheare." With her falls a tear, in its turn metamorphosed into a pearl (one of Carew's favorite images) enclosing the fly's ashes: "Thus she receiv'd from *Celia's* eye, / Funerall flame, tombe, Obsequie" (ll. 19 - 20).

Aside from the difficulty of the female fly as the poet's rival, this poem, in smart tetrameter couplets,[11] demonstrates Carew's abilities within another established genre—the poem dealing with small creatures, also a favorite with Lovelace, and a reminiscence of Martial, Politian, Guarini, and the *Greek Anthology.*[12] The poet becomes so involved in his own cleverness, however, that Celia is almost forgotten, and the poem remains a feat of wit.

In what might easily be described as a companion poem to "A Flye that flew into my Mistris her eye" from the standpoint of theme and versification, a bee[13] has built "her" nest "I' th Hyblas of her [Celia's] either breast" (l. 4). "Swan-like," she has reached her apex of beauty just prior to death (by drowning in water "More precious then the Phaenix fire," l. 14). It seems that the bee has sucked the "Arromattick dew" from the vale between Celia's "two twin-sister hils"; and this "Ambrosiall meat, / A rowling file of Balmy sweat," an image that has been offensive to at least one critic,[14] has brought extinction. Here again, however, Celia has "killed only to be kind," for the "beauty mark" of the title, "Upon a Mole in Celias bosome" (113 - 14), is the metamorphosed bee, immortalized forever[15] through its "shadow" on Celia's "Elizian plaines." Moreover, it becomes for lovers an emblem of the sweetness and dangerousness of love:

Yet still her shaddow there remaines
Confind to those Elizian plaines;
With this strict Law, that who shall lay
His bold lips on that milky way,
The sweet, and smart, from thence shall bring
Of the Bees Honey, and her sting.
                    (ll. 15 - 20)

A similar recognition of the bittersweet nature of love (". . . had not kind Rheume vext me then, / I might not Celia kisse," ll. 3 - 4), as well as of the curative powers of the mistress, is presented in "The tooth-ach cured by a kisse" (109 - 10). The disorder in question is so domestic as to suggest that its poem may be of the stuff of real life. At any rate, physicians become the poet's scorn, for they can but "Patch up a body for a time" (l. 9) ("No more then Chimists can sublime / True Gold, the Indies wealth,"[16] ll. 11 - 12), while Celia's cures are permanent. If their powers are as delimited as those of alchemists, Celia's expand in no mean direction. The "angel of the healing pool" (John 5: 1 - 4) "Hath to her lip the seat of love, / As to his heaven retir'd" (ll. 15 - 16).

Again Carew has tried too hard to ply the Metaphysical yoking of disparate materials (commendation of the mistress, the curing of a toothache, and biblical allusion). There is a skillful alternation of iambic tetrameter and iambic trimeter lines, but the poem is too ingenious, almost a parody of "occasional" verse.

The powers of Celia's voice are extolled in two poems of the same title: "Song. *Celia* singing." In the first (38), which uses tetrameter couplets, she becomes another Orpheus, stilling the wind and making mild the bore and panther[17] with the dual implements of hand and voice. Statues are transformed into men and men into statues. The former, now men, court her with tears, but she is unyielding ("more stony then they were," l. 14) and thus "enstones" them once again. As is often the case with Carew himself (or with his persona in the poems), they are overcome by the paradox of beauty and disdain, a remnant of the sonnet tradition.

The second compliment to Celia's singing (39) forsakes regularity for a combination of iambic tetrameter and iambic dimeter lines, a break in couplet rhyme to emphasize *heare* (l. 5), and truncation (ll. 1, 10). It takes off from the Renaissance cliché of Love entering by sending his dart through the eyes and into the heart.[18] Set to music by Lawes, this poem introduces Celia as a singing siren who proves "That Love can enter at the eare"(l. 9).[19] After the song is finished, the eyes, too, it is promised, will be ravished—by Celia as the sun:

> Then unvaile your eyes, behold
> The curious mould
> Where that voyce dwels, and as we know,
> When the Cocks crow,
> We freely may
> Gaze on the day;
> So may you, when the Musique's done
> Awake and see the rising Sun.
> (ll. 10 - 17)[20]

Despite the derivativeness of the content, the metrical handling and the dangerous but contained intrusion of the analogy of the cock crowing compel the reader's attention.

III   *The Poet's Rival*

Besides the bee and the fly, Carew has a human rival ("To my Rivall," 41) in a rather conventional poem treating secular love in religious terms. The "vaine intruder" is warned not to wash "with thy unhallowed brine / The foot-steps of my *Celia's* shrine" (ll. 2 - 3). His accents may incline a "looser Dame" to love, but Celia "must have offerings more divine":

> Such pearlie drops, as youthfull *May*
> Scatters before the rising day;
>   Such smooth soft language, as each line
> Might stroake an angry God, or stay
>   *Joves* thunder, make the hearers pine
> With envie. . . .
>   (ll. 8 - 13)

While the use of pearls is characteristic of Carew's imagery, there are subtlety and force in the claims made for his poetry (ll. 10 - 13). The impression created is that, if the intruder can write poetry of this caliber, he rightly may take his place as "Servant to her, Rivall with me" (l. 14; presumably as lover *and* poet). Even in a poem less than original in content, the reader is struck by Carew's way with an image: "Such smooth soft language, as each line / Might stroake an angry God." The tetrameter lines, the experimentation within the sonnet form, and the use of alliteration also deserve notice.

IV   *The Unity of the Lovers*

"Celia bleeding, to the Surgeon" (26) attacks the limited powers of the physician in the fashion of "The tooth-ach cured by a kisse" and, like that poem, seems to reflect a true episode subsequently commemorated in ("occasional") poetry. The images are not at all new in Carew's work ("Crystall case," "purple chanels," "azure veines," the "hard rock" repelling the "keenest darts of Love"[21]), but some interest is cultivated by the poet's addressing the "fond" or foolish physician and recording his reply. In addition, the episode nicely prepares for a Donnean notion that becomes Carew's *coup de théâtre* in the third and last stanza:

> But thou reply'st, behold she bleeds;
>   Foole, thou'rt deceivd; and dost not know
> The mystique knot whence this proceeds,
>   How Lovers in each other grow;
> Thou struckst her arme, but 'twas my heart
> Shed all the blood, felt all the smart.[22]

Despite the beauty of that conceit or image of the "mystique knot," the content, like that of "The tooth-ach cured by a kisse" and of those on small creatures, is more contrived than effective. That contrivance is partially undercut, however, by the regularity and grace of the metrical scheme: iambic tetrameter lines in three stanzas rhyming ababcc.

Another apparently true-life situation[23] is dealt with in "Song. To a Lady not yet enjoy'd by her Husband" (36). The hackneyed image of twining eye-beams symbolizing "soules flitting" and "Our loving hearts together knitting"[24] creates an impression of unity between the lovers such that, even at the time when Celia is "enjoy'd by her Husband," their love will endure and thrive. The rare use by Carew of a refrain subtly reiterates the possibility of their relationship enduring beyond Celia's marriage and unites the two against the husband in the classic eternal triangle: "Let Eaglets the bright Sun survey, / Though the blind Mole discerne not day." But the tenuousness of the affair is also projected by the catalectic foot in the second and fourth lines of each of the three stanzas (ababcc), which alter those lines from the dominant tetrameter to pentameter.

The enigmatic[25] second stanza—

> When cleere Aurora leaves her mate,
>   The light of her gray eyes dispising,
> Yet all the world doth celebrate
>   With sacrifice, her faire up-rising:
> Let Eaglets the bright Sun survey,
> Though the blind Mole discerne not day.

—seems to issue in a similar contrast, this time between the grayness of dawn (the ominousness of Celia's marriage) and the brightness it heralds (the indissoluble unity of the lovers). The husband may be (in Stanza 3) the dragon-keeper of the "golden fruit," yet he will never "taste" their love, just as "others pin'd in the pursuit," while only the present speaker has been successful and will continue to be so. When the poet addresses the lady, he lets her think that their love will endure no matter what. When he is realistic, he admits the unlikelihood to himself. The cynicism of the situation penetrates the poem.

V *The Raptures of Their Love*

Celia and the poet not only know the great unity of true love; but, like Donne's lovers in the aftermath of "The Extasie," they can "to bodies" gloriously go. Among Carew's most famous poems and one that established his early reputation as a libertine, "A Rapture" (49 - 53) is still considered by some critics as "for the most part unquotable"[26] and as a deliberate attempt to surpass the Roman and Italian amorists.[27]

It begins its long series of pentameter couplets that spill over into paragraphs with the declaration of enjoying Celia *now*. The remainder of the first verse paragraph is given to convincing her that (personified) Honor is a giant only to the meek. To bold, audacious lovers, he is merely a "masquer"—

> . . . not as we once thought
> The seed of Gods, but a weake modell wrought
> By greedy men, that seeke to enclose the common,
> And within private armes empale free woman.
> (ll. 17 - 20)

The *we* proclaims that the line of reasoning here is hers as well as his. Besides, what woman could possibly accept the loss of her freedom?

The second "paragraph" likewise employs the imperative. "Come now" and they will fly above the "Monsters [Honor's] head" to "Loves Elizium," where the Queen of Love reigns and banishes all offense; in Love's country, Love is Queen, and there can be no question of honor. The wooer imaginatively constructs Love's country as he describes their foreplay, mutual enjoyment, and postorgasmic drowsiness in a Venerian setting (ll. 35 - 38)[28] that will ultimately again (ll. 45 - 54) "Rowze us, and shoot into our

veines fresh fire, / Till we, in their sweet extasie expire" (11. 53 -
54). With remarkable variety (considering the circumstances!), this
second sexual interlude leaves the blazon technique of the first to
adopt the conceit of the bee refurbishing his bag with honey
gathered from a garden of flowers (including "the ripned Cherry").
Since the poem reveals Carew at his most sexually explicit and has,
as much as any other, defined him as a poet, it is worth quoting at
length:

> Then, as the empty Bee, that lately bore,
> Into the common treasure, all her store,
> Flyes 'bout the painted field with nimble wing,
> Deflowring the fresh virgins of the Spring;
> So will I rifle all the sweets, that dwell
> In my delicious Paradise, and swell
> My bagge with honey, drawne forth by the power
> Of fervent kisses, from each spicie flower.
> I'le seize the Rose-buds in their perfum'd bed,
> The Violet knots, like curious Mazes spread
> O're all the Garden, taste the ripned Cherry,
> The warme, firme Apple, tipt with corall berry:
> Then will I visit, with a wandring kisse,
> The vale of Lillies, and the Bower of blisse:
> And where the beauteous Region doth divide
> Into two milkie wayes, my lips shall slide
> Downe those smooth Allies, wearing as I goe
> A tract for lovers on the printed snow. . . .
> (ll. 55 - 72)

The reader is suddenly made to reassess—Carew did not drop the
blazon technique after all; he only decked it in allegory and
Spenserian overtones ("Bower of blisse")! "A Rapture" constantly
surprises and makes one reconsider what has just been read. Finally,
in a masterful mingling of euphemism (Celia's "grove of Eglan-
tine") and alchemical imagery, he will

> . . . all those ravisht sweets distill
> Through Loves Alimbique, and with Chimmique skill
> From the mixt masse, one soveraigne Balme derive,
> Then bring that great *Elixar* to thy hive.
> (ll. 75 - 78)

Another long and concentrated analogy is unfolded in Section 4.
Celia becomes a "sea of milke"; he, the invading, "smooth, calme

Ocean," who then reverts to a tempest comparable to the visitation of Jove upon Danaë. His ship will, however, arrive safely "into Loves channell" with her as pilot; and peace will follow once more.

The remainder of this paragraph and the whole of the fifth are devoted to the theorem that no sins exist in Love's Elysium except those of omission ("when Loves rites are not done," l. 114). The Honor-bound world is reversed here where the only Lucrece (renowned for her chastity), a virtual Lais (a courtesan), is the one in Pietro Aretine's lascivious paintings; where Penelope (renowned for wifely devotion) prefers "th' amorous sport of gamesome nights"; where Daphne rejects her roots and runs to the embraces of Apollo; where Laura lies in Petrarch's arms; and where "ten thousand Beauties more, that dy'de / Slave to the Tyrant [Honor]" "Pay into Loves Exchequer double rent."

Though the fact seems generally to be overlooked by critics, the argument to this point has all been hypothetical, in the speaker's imagination—intended to induce Celia to "enjoy" him now. The last verse paragraph drops its tone to that of practical logic (much the tune, throughout, of Andrew Marvell's "To His Coy Mistress"). The problem is not simply that Honor "fetter[s] your soft sex with Chastitie, / Which Nature made unapt for abstinence" (ll. 152 - 53)—Honor also creates another human paradox. He demands that men fight for the "honor" of their mistresses, "And yet religion bids from blood-shed flye" (l. 163). The bluntness of the poet's conclusion, accordingly, suggests that Celia cannot possibly resurrect any defense of Honor:[29]

> . . . Then tell me why
> This Goblin Honour which the world adores,
> Should make men Atheists, and not women Whores.
> (ll. 164 - 66)

The only way to thrive is through love. Although the poem's majority is given over to the construction of an impossible dream of love,[30] Carew becomes tough and realistic at the end: they *must* love to deal with the paradox that is the human situation. To be religious, he must be a coward; to be "honest," she must have her honor protected by him, and thus she forces him to become an "atheist." If she makes love to him, Honor brands her a whore; but is she not more of a "whore" if she turns him into an atheist defending her honor? Finally, and there is the true wit of the concluding thought, in actuality, she will be no more a "whore" by loving him than he will be an atheist by defending her! The sinuous logic is again reminiscent of Donne, especially in a poem like "The Flea."

One other crucial point is made by "A Rapture," which is usually interpreted as merely libertine, naturalistic, and physical.[31] While it well demonstrates what happens when "souls to bodies go," it does not entirely omit the soul. At first the lovers' souls, true, do not mingle: "And so our soules that cannot be embrac'd, / Shall the embraces of our bodyes taste" (11. 43 - 44). But, as with Donne, the bodies "did us to us at first convey," for a *murmur of their souls* wakes the pair to renewed physical bliss (11. 51 - 53). Ultimately, their union would produce, in the golden world of love at least, the halcyon calm and security that are the marks of Donne's higher love and that partake of the same Donnean application of religious images to secular love:

> Then shall thy circling armes, embrace and clip
> My willing bodie, and thy balmie lip
> Bathe me in juyce of kisses, whose perfume
> Like a religious incense shall consume,
> And send up holy vapours, to those powres
> That blesse our loves, and crowne our sportfull houres,
> That with such Halcion calmenesse, fix our soules
> In steadfast peace, as no affright controules.
> (ll. 91 - 98)

The only escape from an Honor-driven world is the golden fabrication constructed by the poet's pen. The very fact that the golden world is drawn by tough and intellectual means insists that, for the speaker at least, the reality of bodies cannot be denied. The verse, like that reality, is not liquid-smooth and graceful.

VI   *His Declaration of Eternal Love*

In "The protestation, a Sonnet" (109), Carew turns back to the "impossibilities" theme and to the Petrarchan claim that the only true love is that which endures.[32] Each of the four stanzas of six tetrameter lines and, curiously, rhyming couplets, cites impossible changes that will result if the poet forsakes Celia: for example, "The fish shall in the Ocean burne" (1.7), "Blacke *Laethe* shall oblivion leave" (l. 11), "Love shall his bow and shaft lay by" (l. 13), and "Grim death no more shall horrid prove" (l. 23).

All in all, the poem is among Carew's least original, as if his practicality would not permit a great expenditure of effort on such a trifling stand. The most competent stanza is the first with its capturing of the spring season that is Love's best:

> No more shall meads be deckt with flowers,
> Nor sweetnesse dwell in rosie bowers:
> Nor greenest buds on branches spring,
> Nor warbling birds delight to sing,
> Nor Aprill violets paint the grove,
> If I forsake my *Celias* love.

Inevitably, the reader recalls the cynical pointing Donne has given the impossibilities theme in "Song" ("Go and Catch a Falling Star"). So often is there a similar kind of twist or barb in Carew's poetry that one feels restless before the cloyed sweetness of "The protestation, a Sonnet."

VII *Advice to Other Lovers Wooing Other Celias*

A similar derivativeness[33] seems at first reading to pervade "Boldnesse in love" (42), in some manuscripts called "The Marigold." The traditional emblem of the marigold unfolding to and following the sun becomes an object-lesson for a lover trying to master the art of wooing his own "Celia":

> Marke how the bashfull morne, in vaine
> Courts the amorous Marigold,
> With sighing blasts, and weeping raine;
> Yet she refuses to unfold,
> But when the Planet of the day,
> Approacheth with his powerfull ray,
> Then she spreads, then she receives
> His warmer beames into her virgin leaves.
> So shalt thou thrive in love, fond Boy;
> If thy teares, and sighes discover
> Thy griefe, thou never shalt enjoy
> The just reward of a bold lover. . . .
> (ll. 1 - 12)

Speaking from his experience with Celia, the poet brings development to the emblem. In the first place, he has the "bashfull morne" court the flower in vain "With sighing blasts, and weeping raine," analogues for the ploys of the sonnet lover. The case is quite different, on the other hand, for the sun "with his powerful ray."

Thus the "fond Boy" who seeks to master the art of courtship must not let his lady witness his tears and sighs, but must act the "bold lover":

> But when with moving accents, thou
> Shalt constant faith, and service vow,
> Thy *Celia* shall receive those charmes
> With open eares, and with unfolded armes.
>   (ll. 13 - 16)

Carew's originality here is the subtle emphasis again on the power of poetry. The foolish boy is likely to leave naively confident, totally innocent of the real message he has heard: the lover who would succeed must be a true *poet!* The boldness of the *poet*-lover is demonstrated by the shift from tetrameter to pentameter lines in 8 and 16, the use of a catalectic fifth foot in l. 12, and the use of a truncated fourth foot in l. 7.

VIII   *Insufficiency of Love, Insufficiency of Disdain*

Despite his stance of authority and experience in the previous poem, Carew has his own troubles with his Celia. In what is apparently a colloquy with himself, "Griefe ingrost" (44 - 45), his more rational side asks why he is writing such complaining, sad poems while she continues to "disdaine." He can exact his revenge by dying and thereby killing her through the cessation of the verses that make her live:

> Wherefore doe thy sad numbers flow
>   So full of woe?
> Why dost thou melt in such soft straines,
>   Whilst she disdaines?
>   If she must still denie,
>   Weepe not, but dye:
>   And in thy Funerall fire,
>   Shall all her fame expire.
> Thus both shall perish, and as thou on thy Hearse
> Shall want her teares, so she shall want thy Verse;
>   Repine not then at thy blest state:
>   Thou art above thy fate. . . .
>   (ll. 1 - 12)

The languish self, however, must relinquish the logic of this advice, for

> . . . my faire *Celia* will nor give
> Love enough to make me live,
> Nor yet dart from her eye
> Scorne enough to make me dye.
>   (ll. 13 - 16)

This hateful "seige of contraries," from the Elizabethan sonnet tradition, this detested state of being trapped "in-between," a popular theme with Carew,[34] forces him to resolve to "weepe alone" until she either makes him totally happy or kills him with coldness.

Strangely, while the content of the poem is derivative and perfunctory, the prosody is among Carew's most interesting. He combines tetrameter, dimeter, trimeter, and pentameter lines and uses two truncated feet (ll. 14 and 16) and one catalectic foot (converting l. 9 to a hexameter line or a catalectic Alexandrine). He uses all of this variation and yet his customary couplet rhyming. As a lyrical poem should, Carew's "Griefe ingrost" describes an emotional crisis of the singer-poet, here most effectively through the changes of the metrical system. Again Celia becomes less important than she perhaps should as the verse itself becomes so intricate.

IX   *The Trials of Love*

Carew and Celia seem indeed to have had their share of the progressive disorders of love. In the three six-line tetrameter stanzas (ababcc) of "Ingratefull beauty threatned" (17 - 18), he "blackmails" her back within the confines of the affair. She has been "proud" and has tempted him with "affrights," and he now uses the favorite Renaissance theme of immortality through poetry to browbeat her into conformity. His verse has given her renown, singled her out from "common beauties," "ympt the wings of fame," and given her voice and eyes "That killing power." She shines in *his* skies, yet has dared "dart . . . from thy borrowed sphere / Lightning on him that fixt thee there" (ll. 11 - 12). The wise poet, however, knows his own creation:

> Let fooles thy mystique formes adore,
>   I'le know thee in thy mortall state:
> Wise Poets that wrap't Truth in tales,
> Knew her themselves, through all her vailes.
>   (ll. 15 - 18)

This poem is among Carew's most representative;[35] in it he is the smooth love poet mingling Classical, Italian, French, and contemporary influences: the Roman poet Propertius, Francesco Petrarch, Pierre de Ronsard, and John Donne and Ben Jonson,[36] respectively.

Apparently, the "blackmail" of "Ingratefull beauty threatned" is ineffective, and so "A deposition from Love" (16 - 17) must lament Celia's actual breach of faith in three ten-line stanzas[37] (ababcdcdee, with alternating tetrameter and trimeter lines) that combine stock materials: especially legal images and the Petrarchan conceit of the besieged fort.[38] Warned against women, the speaker nonetheless admits that he foolishly imagined that a lover, after a certain trial of pain, would surely take the "fortress" and gain the "Paradise within": "I thought loves plagues, like Dragons sate, / Only to fright us at the gate" (ll. 9 - 10). And so he conquered and loved in the grand and best tradition of "Come live with me, and be my love." Perhaps drawing on the topos that the worst is the remembrance of past happiness, he suggests that "*Jove* were too meane a guest" at the height of their love and goes on to expand the analogy beyond its usual limits:

> If the stout Foe will not resigne,
>   When I besiege a Towne,
> I lose, but what was never mine;
>   But he that is cast downe
> From enjoy'd beautie, feeles a woe,
> Onely deposed Kings can know.
>   (ll. 25 - 30)

While Carew did not live to see the outbreak of the Civil War, he shows his strong Royalism here in the prophetic image of fellow-feeling with a deposed king. Perhaps the poem is a reaction to Celia's marriage.

The poem's achievement is its success in turning the stock materials into an occasion for philosophical rumination. The movement is sure: I thought; I did; I lost and think again.

"To Celia, upon Love's Ubiquity" (123 - 24) is Carew's presentation of the "unhappy-with-her, unhappy-without-her" theme. He opens with two similes meant to demonstrate his sense of loss. He is like a sick man striving to get his breath by changing places; he is like a ball filled with fire and powder.

> I restles am, yet live, each minute kild,
> And with that moving torture must retain
> (With change of all things else) a constant payn.
>   (ll. 8 - 10)

If he goes to Holland, France, or India, he changes "onely Coun-
treys not my mind" (l. 16), and "Despair and hopeless fate still
follow me" (l. 18). Conventionally, the sea becomes the emblem of
his own troubled fate; the skies recall Celia's eyes—"All things but
make me mind my business, you" (l. 28). In a Donnean[39] image, the
compass, though its motivation is quite different from that of "A
Valediction: Forbidding Mourning," he proclaims his chains:

> My whole life is bout you, the Center starre,
> But a perpetuall Motion Circular:
> I am the dyalls hand, still walking round,
> You are the Compasse, and I never sound
> Beyond your Circle, neyther can I shew
> Ought, but what first expressed is in you:
> That wheresoever my teares doe cause me move
> My fate still keepes me bounded with your love;
> Which ere it dye, or be extinct in me,
> Time shall stand still, and moist waves flaming be.
>
> (ll. 33 - 42)

He has declared the eternality of his love and has dipped into the
Petrarchan "impossibilities" motif once again. The last lines also express a conventional thought to close the poem far less satisfactorily
than it has begun: "But when I dye, and wish all comforts
given, / Ile think on you, and by you think on heaven."

"To Celia, upon Love's Ubiquity" is not one of the poems in
which Carew so gracefully manages to reinvigorate tired materials.
From l. 7 to its end, it is hardly more than a series of hackneyed images in largely uninspired pentameter couplets. Yet the first six lines
have impressively captured the sensation of the lover's restlessness.
One has the impression that Carew lost his original burst of inspiration. Unfortunately, because of the compass image, critics often use
this poem to contrast Carew's technique with Donne's.

Another poem reveals that "straying," one of the frequent trials
of love, can be a two-fold game. While the lady remains unidentified, Carew's address "To T. H. a Lady resembling my Mistresse"
(26 - 27) indicates that he could pay court to others and that he was
well known as the devotee of "Celia." Echoes of Donne (especially
the coinage conceit of the last four stanzas) are present, as well as
images used with some frequency in other Carew poems (e.g.,
"nest"); but the significant tone is one of the quiet exercising of
logic[40] that often appears in Carew's poems:

> Disdaine not a divided heart,
> Though all be hers, you shall have part;
> Love is not tyde to rules of art.
>
> For as my soule first to her flew,
> Yet stay'd with me; so now 'tis true
> It dwells with her, though fled to you.
>   (ll. 4 - 9)

Through the whole, he manages to convey a sense of being totally candid with both ladies. When "T. H." reminds him of Celia's prior claim, he skillfully uses that claim for leverage, giving every appearance of fair dealing:

> So though all other hearts resigne
> To your pure worth, yet you have mine
> Only because you are her coyne.
>   (ll. 25 - 27)

Tired of "T. H.'s" quibbles, he uses some equivocations of his own; she is not likely to be pleased with the sentiments, but has "asked for them." Praised for her "pure worth" or not, T. H. is not likely to forget the sting of the last two lines.

The poem is worth examining because the relationship to Donne is more worthy of Carew than that in "To Celia, upon Love's Ubiquity." Also, Carew's form here is the tercet (aaa); for all the logic and precision of the arguments, the tetrameter tercets make the poem sing.

Celia's disdain ultimately triggers in the poet "Disdaine returned" (18), one of Carew's best-known poems. He again uses the six-line stanza (ababcc) in tetrameters but extends the third and last stanza by a couplet stating the poem's resolution. As if to emphasize his resolution, that couplet contains the only lines that do not display either truncation or catalexis.

The first stanza is *carpe diem* once again, though declarative and practical here rather than hortative. The poet-lover's philosophy, seen also in other poems, is set forth in Stanza 2—eternal love results from love of "a smooth, and stedfast mind" and is an "equall love." "Where these are not, I despise / Lovely cheekes, or lips, or eyes." The third stanza, though often omitted,[41] produces the fit between poem and title. Celia may importune, but in vain. He has searched her "soule within, / And find[s] nought, but pride, and scorne." Poetic justice now demands that his revenge be satisfied by transferring to her the hopeless love that he is casting away.[42]

X *Parting*

"Parting, Celia weepes" (48 - 49) seems to commemorate a separation of the lovers for a limited period.[43] It too strikes a note of logic similar to that of Donne's "A Valediction: Forbidding Mourning." Both poems attempt to involve the lady's mind so that she at least momentarily may cast off grief by the rerouting of her thoughts. Carew's Celia is requested not to weep and add her "heavinesse" to his: logically, "Since Fate our pleasures must disjoyne, / Why should our sorrowes meet?" (ll. 4 - 5). Further, his grief will be relieved "to thinke thou dost not grieve" (l. 8). On the other hand, Celia should weep, for thus he can transport her sighs and tears with him ". . . so shall thy brest / And eyes discharg'd, enjoy their rest" (ll. 11 - 12). Besides, ". . . it will glad my heart to see, / Thou wer't thus loath to part with mee" (ll. 13 - 14). A reading of the entire poem produces just this sense of "connectives" from thought to thought.

Attempting to disengage her thoughts from the sorrows of parting, he gives every impression that he has engaged his own as he darts from related thought to related thought throughout the whole. It is precisely his capturing of "thought in motion" that prevents the poem from becoming a slim production indeed. Despite the facile couplets, in tetrameters, Carew produces the effect of being overtaken by an intellectual process himself. Once again, Celia recedes into the background as the speaker becomes totally engrossed by his own progressively unfolding logic. Occasionally, the reader feels that Carew had rather write something other than conventional love poetry.

The parting of "To his mistris" (121) knells their final separation, probably as a result of Celia's marriage ("the fury of thy fate"?), though Carew has hoped, in "To a Lady not yet enjoy'd by her Husband," for a continuation of their relationship beyond that fatal event. He enjoins her not to grieve, but to hasten to her fate. Like Donne's lovers who would keep the "laity" at a distance, he reminds Celia: " 'Tis some perfection to waste / Discreetly out our wretched state" (ll. 3 - 4). Perhaps their braveness and stoical fortitude will win a concession from Destiny:

> Who knowes but destiny may relent,
> For many miracles have bin,
> Thou proving thus obedient
>   To all the griefs she plundgd thee in?
> And then the certainty she meant
> Reverted is by accident.
>   (ll. 7 - 12)

By Stanza 3, however, he is forced to admit how great is the grief, even though, curiously, human love never can be perfect:

> But yet I must confesse tis much
> When we remember what hath bin,
> Thus parting never more to touch
>   To let eternall absence in,
> Though never was our pleasure yet
> So pure, but chance distracted it.
>   (ll. 13 - 18)

As if in reaction to his own allowed taint of imperfection, he challenges her not to submit to Fate "And dye to one anothers love" (ll. 19 - 20). The four six-line stanzas (ababcc, in tetrameters) have a final pentameter couplet as a coda. This coda states the lovers' course philosophically and universally. Their bodies may be parted, but true love can be destroyed only by themselves:[44] "Fate and the Planets sometymes bodies part, / But Cankerd nature onely alters th' heart." If this poem does herald the physical separation of Carew and Celia, the affair was resolved with amazing amicability, the admission of imperfection in their love being perhaps the instrument of inducing objectivity in both.

CHAPTER 3

The Love Poems Not Addressed to Celia

I   Poems to Carew's Mistress

A.   "Autobiographical" Poems to His Mistress

L IKE some of Carew's Celia poems, six of the poems directed to the more generalized "mistress" suggest autobiographical episodes. Of them, "Upon some alterations in my Mistresse, after my departure into France" (24 - 25), which apparently refers to the period of his service with Sir Edward Herbert, is one of the few Carew poems to be dated with any certainty.

He plays on Petrarchan conventions with himself as the despairing lover, "a fraile Barke," tossed on an angry sea "Of ruthlesse pride," "Gulfes of disdaine," "shifting sands/Of faithlesse love, and false inconstancie," and "rocks of crueltie" (Stanza 1). As expected, his "sighs have rays'd those winds" (1. 12), yet the extensiveness of Carew's treatment transforms these trite materials. Especially fine is the picture he paints in the final lines:

> A mystie cloud of anger, hides the light
> Of my faire starre, and every where black night
> Usurpes the place
> Of those bright rayes, which once did grace
> My forth-bound Ship: but when it could no more
> Behold the vanisht shore,
> In the deep flood she drown'd her beamie face.
> (ll. 16 - 22)

The characteristic Carew touch is the concentration on and development of the image, regardless of its source, once a definite selection has been made. Also worth noticing are the metrical

variations, chosen perhaps to emphasize the changes in his mistress.
The two eleven-line stanzas are in rhyming couplets except for the
unrhymed last line. The line length varies from pentameter (ll. 1, 2,
4 - 6, 9, and 11) to dimeter (ll. 3 and 7) to tetrameter (l. 8) to
trimeter (ll. 2 and 10). As in "Loves Courtship," Carew seems conscious of form as meaning.

Another sea analogy, equally hackneyed, opens "My mistris commanding me to returne her letters" (9 - 11), perhaps also written
while Carew was in France. The returning of her letters is as
grievous to him as would be to a merchant the expedient of casting
his goods overboard in a storm. But he must obey her to the death;
and, since only the letters and not he must touch her hands, he *will*
die (ll. 1 - 10).

The opening lines demonstrate a feature of many Carew poems.
Despite the couplet rhyming of the pentameters, the reader hears a
real person speak and *think* as he speaks. The lines spill over into
long sentences; group adjectives (as "long-toiled-for treasure") are
rather common. Such examples stand out from the crisp, polished,
"gem-like" poems that are among the widely known of his works.
Yet, at their best, the reader would not want any further polishing
of this group, any lessening of the feeling that this is the way a
man's mind works—anywhere, not just in poetry.

As they learn they are to be sent "Home to their native soile from
banishment" (l. 12), the letters smile, "like dying Saints, that
know / They are to leave the earth, and tow'rd heaven goe" (ll. 13 -
14). The poet instructs them in what to say when they arrive,
culminating in a request that, in exchange for them, she send him
her heart. If she refuses, he will lay his case before the God of Love.
He begins to practice his "brief" now. First comes the recital of his
progress in love in conventional martial rhetoric and great detail:

> Trav'ling thy Countries road (*great God*) I spide
> By chance this Lady, and walkt by her side
> From place, to place, fearing no violence,
> For I was well arm'd, and had made defence
> In former fights, 'gainst fiercer foes, then shee
> Did at our first incounter seeme to bee.
> But going farther, every step reveal'd
> Some hidden weapon, till that time conceal'd.
> Seeing those outward armes, I did begin
> To feare, some greater strength was lodg'd within.
> Looking into her mind, I might survay

> An hoast of beauties that in ambush lay;
> And won the day before they fought the field;
> For I unable to resist, did yeild.
>   (ll. 33 - 46)

He had won other and fiercer fights and so thought to triumph; but, once again complementing the spiritual with the physical, he failed to reckon with her secret strength, the "hoast of beauties" in her mind. Finally vanquished, he is left bleeding from a "heart wound," which festers within, though "two cunning Leaches," absence and time, have drawn the flesh together. The "en-ditement" at length draws to a close. If she has been frightened by this recital of the charges against her, she can return his heart. But, if she cannot find it ("for perhaps it may / Mong'st other trifeling hearts be out oth' way," ll. 77 - 78), "Bid her but send me hers, and we are friends" (l. 80).

In spite of the clever turn of the ending and the achievement of a conversational tone, this surely is one of Carew's most laborious poems, really a compendium of Petrarchan clichés, though the various frames (the merchant simile, the conceit of the "war of love," the invocation of the God of Love, and the address to the letters) into which they are placed exert some appeal by their extensive development and richness of detail.

Quite different is the very Donnean "To my Mistresse in absence" (22), which, while it may refer to a particular episode (even Carew's sojourn in France again), seems less "personal." Though the speaker is gone, his mind and heart remain within the beloved ("Twas but a carkasse that did part," l. 6). In tones reminiscent of Donne's "The Extasie," he requests that she allow their spirits to mingle. The "mystique wreath" is not this time another Donnean "bracelet of bright hair about the bone" but mingling souls:

> Yet let our boundlesse spirits meet,
> And in loves spheare each other greet;
> There let us worke a mystique wreath,
> Unknowne unto the world beneath;
> There let our claspt loves sweetly twin;
> There let our secret thoughts unseen,
> Like nets be weav'd, and inter-twin'd,
> Wherewith wee'le catch each others mind:
> There whilst our soules doe sit and kisse,

> Tasting a sweet, and subtle blisse,
> (Such as grosse lovers cannot know,
> Whose hands, and lips, meet here below;)
> Let us looke downe, and marke what paine
> Our absent bodyes here sustaine. . . .
>   (ll. 9 - 22)

Like Donne also, Carew sees his mistress and himself as keeping out
the "laity" of love—"grosse lovers." More characteristic of Carew
than of Donne, however, is the stress on *mutual* love and the vision
of the souls themselves enjoying love:

> There let us joy to see from farre,
> Our emulous flames at loving warre,
> Whilst both with equall luster shine,
> Mine bright as yours, yours bright as mine.
> There seated in those heavenly bowers,
> Wee'le cheat the lag, and lingring houres,
> Making our bitter absence sweet,
> Till soules, and bodyes both, may meet.
>   (ll. 27 - 34)

Nonetheless, like Donne's lovers, they anticipate "going to bodies."
  This poem assumes a less personal quality than "My mistris commanding me to returne her letters" because of the very smoothness
of its polished tetrameter couplets and because the speaker finally
ignores the crisis brought on by his mistress ("Though I must live
here, and by force / Of your command suffer divorce," ll. 1 - 2) and
spends the poem imagining the mingling of their souls. After the
opening, he no longer acknowledges that she has sent him away but
indulges in fantasies about *the* perfect love, not *their* perfect love.
As a result, the poem is far more interesting for its glimpse of the
speaker than as another "document" in the quest for the elusive
woman of Carew's life.
  Two rather humorous poems show Carew back in the mundane
world, though the first, "Song. To one that desired to know my
Mistris" (39 - 40), indulges equally in pipe dreams and in the
proverbial "knocking on wood." There is no need for his rival to
know his mistress—one wonders if Carew might ironically be using
the biblical *know*—for she "Hath vow'd her constant faith to me"
(1. 2). Mild to him, she will be only "stormy" to the intruder:

> For if her beautie stirre desire
> In me, her kisses quench the fire.
> Or, I can to Love's fountaine goe,

> Or dwell upon her hills of snow;
> But when thou burn'st, she shall not spare
> One gentle breath to coole the ayre;
> Thou shalt not climbe those Alpes, nor spye
> Where the sweet springs of Venus lye.
>   (ll. 5 - 12)

Then, in an echo, though less exasperated, of the opening of Donne's "The Canonization," he urges:

> Search hidden Nature, and there find
> A treasure to inrich thy mind;
> Discover Arts not yet reveal'd,
> But let my Mistris live conceal'd. . . .
>   (ll. 13 - 16)

He rounds off the performance with one of his sententious final couplets: "Though men by knowledge wiser grow, / Yet here 'tis wisdome not to know."

The impression created is again of a focus principally on the speaker himself. Like an average person faced with the possibility of a rival, he has reassured himself that all is well by constructing an image of his love more perfect than actual. It is precisely such posturing by Carew (or perhaps by the "persona") that lifts the love poems beyond the Petrarchan levels they only seem to seek. The process is akin to that of Donne in "The Triple Foole." The tetrameter couplets are more liquid than any of Donne's poetry, however.

The second poem, "Song. To one who when I prais'd my Mistris beautie, said I was blind" (33), is more humorous and makes one wonder just how valid the poet's judgment of beauty is. Carew must have enjoyed writing the title as well as the poem.

It makes skillful use of such standbys as "powerfull beames that flye / From her eye" (1. 6) and "those amorous sweets that lye / Scatter'd, in each neighbouring part" (11. 8 - 9). The joke is turned finally on the detractor. If lucky enough to discover her graces, he will be blinded as the speaker is—i.e., "dazel'd." On the other hand, ". . . if those beauties you not spy, / Then are you blinder farre then I."

Such poems as this have earned Carew the reputation of being a "clever" and, unfortunately, a "slender" poet. Judgment should be withheld until he is seen in all of his moods. Even the switch from tetrameter to dimeter (in ll. 2, 4, and 7) and the truncation and catalexis (the latter altering ll. 13 and 14 to pentameter) do not prevent the whole from seeming facile.

A final "autobiographical" poem, "To his jealous Mistris" (110), returns to three regular six-line stanzas (ababcc, in tetrameters). The first line is reassuring as it salutes her with "thou darling of mine eyes." She has, it seems, been taken in by a ruse they formerly used, at *her* suggestion, to keep their affair secret. She has found him paying suit to another in public. Indirectly calling her tears "childish," he vows "henceforth [to] kneele at ne're a shrine, / To blind the world, but only thine" (ll. 17 - 18). While the whole sounds sincere enough, one wonders, given the unveiling of the lover in other poems, whether their "mask" is not doubly beneficial for him.

B. *Commendations of His Mistress*

Four poems to Carew's mistress are purely commendatory. She is so worthy of praise and so beautiful in general, so divine in particular, that he is her "willing prisoner."

The opening line of "In praise of his Mistris" (122), "You, that will a wonder know," might well refer to the whole poem. It is a mild blazon in five six-line stanzas (ababcc, with tetrameter and dimeter lines and much truncation), but with some inflections unusual in Carew. Her eyes are "Two suns in a heaven of snow" (l. 3); her lips are "Leaves of Crimson Tulips [a groan-producing pun!] met" (l. 7), while

> Hills of Milk with Azure mixd
> Swell beneath,
> Waving sweetly, yet still fixd,
> While she doth breath.
> From those hils descends a valley
> Where all fall, that dare to dally.
> (ll. 13 - 18)

But it is the description of her legs that raises the hackles of Edward Selig's critical sensibilities:[1]

> As far Pillars under-stand
> Statues two,
> Whiter than the Silver swan
> That swims in *Poe*;
> If at any tyme they move her
> Every step begets a Lover.
> (ll. 19 - 24)

Still, after the exaggeration and overexuberance, Carew beats a quieter retreat to a trusted image (casket and jewel) and to the old, doting contrast between outer and inner perfections (ll. 25 - 30).

Quite different is another poem of praise, "Song. A beautifull Mistris" (7).[2] Virtually a translation of Giambattista Marino, set to music by Lawes, and another toying with the insuperable brightness of the lady's eyes, it nonetheless shows Carew's power to infuse the conventional with new spirit. The poem is a good specimen of Carew's simple, affecting pictures, set in finely honed verse (tetrameter and dimeter lines with couplet rhyme).

The mellow beauty and "golden" poetry of "A beautiful Mistris" give way to the mild irony more typical of Carew in "A divine Mistris" (6 - 7). The opening promises hyperbolical commendation: the poet always sees "In natures peeces" some need for correction; but his mistress, "fram'd by hands farre more divine," already "hath every beauteous line" (ll. 5 - 6). The middle lines of the poem continue to put the reader off guard, for Carew takes the established view that likeness produces love and thus wishes that Nature, which made him, had created her, too: "Then likenes, might (that loves creates) / Have made her love what now she hates" (ll. 9 - 10). The smooth cadences (rhyming tetrameter couplets) and the sweetness of the thought have left the reader unprepared for the barb, which comes, once again, in the final (pentameter) couplet:[3] "Shee hath too much divinity for mee, / You Gods teach her some more humanitie." The praise was not unadultered after all, and so the charge of extravagance must be retrieved.

Drawing on a tradition that includes Propertius and Pontus de Tyard, and that Carew himself had used in "A Pastorall Dialogue" (42 - 44), the poet next accedes to the powers of his mistress in "Song. The willing Prisoner to his Mistris" (37). Only fools disdain "Cupids yoake" when it is borne by a goddess whose lips unlock a "pearly row" (l. 11). Carew shows his particular fondness for the imagery of pearls and for the oxymóra that are the stock property of the sonnet lover—"ruine, that repaires" (l. 7); "sweet afflictions" (l. 8). The poem is definitely not in Carew's best manner, for it stands in contrast to verses that achieve originality within similarly borrowed frames. The heroic or elegiac quatrains (abab, in tetrameters and pentameters with some catalectic feet) take on a singsong effect unusual in Carew's verse.

C. *The Disdainful Mistress*

The commendations are slightly outnumbered by Carew's ac-

cusations that his mistress is "disdainful." "A cruell Mistris" (8), for
example, builds from a series of antitheses that simultaneously
praise and accuse her. She is the equal of the gods, but her spirit
stands in opposition to theirs. Some kings and some gods have
accepted water from the brook; she will not accept his "rivers of
teares" (ll. 1 - 4). Other gods accept sacrificial animals; "But shee
disdaines the spotlesse sacrifice / Of a pure heart that at her altar
lyes" (ll. 5 - 8). And so on.

The pentameter couplets of the poem are at once more fanciful
and more intricate than a surface reading suggests (though some of
the off-rhymes seem forced). With the exception of the opening
"water" analogy, all of the contrasts relate to fire. By not accepting
his "tears" and thus *him* in mutual love, she burns up, "consumes
her owne Idolater" (l. 16). But his revenge, similar to that exacted
in other poems (e.g., "Ingratefull beauty threatned," 17 - 18;
"Griefe ingrost," 44 - 45), is that, in destroying him, she destroys
herself as she is relegated to oblivion—another example of that
wrenching final couplet for which Carew should be better known:
"Of such a Goddesse no times leave record, / That burnt the temple where she was ador'd." Under the (small) "allegory" of goddess
and devotee, he has once again been talking of the relation between
a poet and his materials; and, though she may be a "goddess" (and
then again, may not be one), the poet / lover *is* a "temple."

One of Carew's best poems, "Song. To my inconstant Mistris"
(15 - 16), influenced by the Roman poets Catullus and Propertius
and by Donne's analogy between religious and secular love, belongs
in the group. The three five-line stanzas (ababb, in tetrameters) are
not only polished; they forcefully drive home the lover's claim:
when she sees his reward for constancy (Stanza 1), another and
better mistress (Stanza 2), she will curse her own failure to treat him
properly (Stanza 3).

The wounded lover[4] begins and ends on the same note: the mistress is a "poore excommunicate" who will be "Damn'd for thy false
Apostasie." He, on the other hand, will receive his "full reward, and
glorious fate" for his "strong faith" in the religion of love, going on
to be cured by a "fayrer hand then thine" and "a soule more pure."
In this "shrug put to music,"[5] "Inconstancy is . . . met with the
threat of counter-inconstancy; and all the rich religious terms take
on in the end a swagger of bravado. The poem thus presents a brief
episode in erotic frustration, a vignette in which the backlash of the
lover's bitterness is conveyed by the immediacy of his language, by

the conversational flexibility of actual speech working within a strict stanza-form."[6] It is this added complexity that enables "To my inconstant Mistris" to soar above the tiredly plaintive notes of the "religion of love."

Elsewhere Carew uses cool logic rather than bitter mocking to meet the lady's cruelty. "Song. To my Mistris, I burning in love" (34) finds him once more trapped in one of the disorders of the unrequited Petrarchan lover. She is silly to think she can quench his flames with disdain. The "sparkles of her eyes" kindled them in the first place, and "What bootes it me, though now you shrowde / Those fierce Comets in a cloude?" (ll. 5 - 6). Her "snow"—"though you should take / Alpes into your bosome" (ll. 9 - 10)!—can never slake his heat. This time the pithy couplet ending is expanded to a renewed lesson in Love's ways. As in, for example, "To my Mistresse in absence" (22), the only answer is equal love:

> But with wonder learne Loves art!
> No seaes of yce can coole desire,
> Equall flames must quench Loves fire:
> Then thinke not that my heat can dye,
> Till you burne aswell as I.
>
> (ll. 12 - 16)

Not particularly distinguished through its content or its tetrameter couplets (though there is interesting truncation in alternate lines), "To my Mistris, I burning in love" does reveal the logical tone Carew likes to assume as he argues the platitudes of love.

The lover learns the perils of logic in a companion piece to the former poem. In "Song. To her againe, she burning in a Feaver" (34 - 35), though it is not addressed directly to his mistress, he discovers that he has not covered all of the contingencies of the argument outlined in that first poem. Now she does burn equally (more, *she* says), but with fever, not love; he is back where he started and can only intone: "Love; let her know the difference / Twixt the heat of soule, and sence" (ll. 11 - 12). Again, the merit of the little poem (in tetrameter couplets with some truncation) falls in the portrayal of the persona as an enthralled lover still capable of a playful self-mockery.

Carew courts the lady once more with logic in "On his Mistres lookeinge in a glasse" (132). The mirror that wears her "shaddow" (actually a "sunne" because of her brightness) reveals itself to be his metamorphosed tears. They have made a circle about her cold heart "where the brinie lake / Congeal'd into a Christall cake" (ll. 5 - 6). Now both glass and shadow / image become emblems of the ravages of time that will overtake her unless she is saved by the immortalizing poetic powers of the pleader.[7]

The only rather unusual feature here is the adoption of tetrameter tercets (aaa). The crystal images recur in Carew's poetry. The poet's pursuit of his argument soon outdistances the compliments to the mistress and leaves the reader once more with the impression that Carew would have preferred most of the time to follow the "masculine line" of Donne.

"To his mistresse retiring in affection" (129 - 30) also enlists the aid of logic, as well as one of Carew's favorite arguments, that only like things are capable of love. He is able, however, to make clever use even of the lady's movement away from him. They are alike and she not only forces Nature by this retrogression (of movement and disdain), but causes a similar disruption within him, an opposition between his affections (which must continue to love her) and his reason (which counsels his own escape from an object he cannot possibly possess).

The poem has a forceful final couplet (altering the pentameters to hexameters by catalexis, as in lines 5 and 6) and again produces a speaking voice who thinks aloud and adopts a stance of reasoning. It is also worth attention for the turn it gives to the "exchange of eyes" conceit. His eyes have made the first movement, but they would not have continued the quest without her responsiveness: "When first mine eyes threw flames, whose spirit moov'd thee / Had'st not thou look't againe I had not lov'd thee."

D. Persuasions to Love

All of these "disdains" should be unnecessary, of course, from the male point of view. And, indeed, the baits of love are beautifully appointed in "To my Mistris sitting by a Rivers side. An Eddy" (14), which is based on Donne's "Elegie VI" and which Edward Selig has used as representative of Carew's poetry.[8] The twenty-six lines of tetrameter couplets are broken into two verse paragraphs. The first (ll. 1 - 18) sets up an analogy between the courtship of the eddy and the bank of the bay into which "she" steals and that of the poet and his mistress. Implicit here is Carew's belief in "equall" love, for the female eddy does most of the wooing and indulges in the coyness of seventeenth-century ladies:

> Marke how she courts the bankes, whilst they
> As amorously their armes display,
> T'embrace, and clip her silver waves:
> See how she strokes their sides, and craves
> An entrance there, which they deny;
> Whereat she frownes, threatning to flye
> Home to her streame, and 'gins to swim
> Backward, but from the chanels brim,
> Smiling, returnes into the creeke,
> With thousand dimples on her cheeke.
> > (ll. 9 - 18)

The second paragraph points the lessons and promises, in beautiful terms, the security and richness of eternal love. This time, perhaps because Carew has drawn the analogy at such length and has so wittily painted the courtship between the eddy and the bank, he does not seem self-conscious:

> Be thou this Eddy, and I'le make
> My breast thy shore, where thou shalt take
> Secure repose, and never dreame
> Of the quite forsaken streame. . . .
> > (ll. 19 - 22)[9]

Derived itself, the water image nevertheless comes off as infinitely less contrived than that of "To her in absence. A Ship" (23) and "Upon some alterations in my Mistresse, after my departure into France" (24 - 25).

II   *Miscellaneous Love Poems*

A.   *Commendatory Poems*

The same crystalline beauty prevails in what is probably Carew's most famous poem, "A Song" (102), "Aske me no more where Jove bestowes." This, with the elegy on John Donne, has received more critical comment than any other Carew poem. It exists in several versions in the manuscripts of Carew's verses and has been imitated and parodied many times, even providing the format for a political song.[10] Through Donne's influence, Carew includes abstruse matters (the philosophical "formal causes") in a love poem; through Jonson's influence, he treats love with orderly and crisp beauty (in tetrameter quatrains).

Always preferring the imperative as his gambit, Carew uses it here in a refrainlike variation for the first line of each of the five stanzas. The first two lines (aa) of a stanza pose a "problem" for which the answer is provided in the last two lines (bb). The whole is a refreshing play on the consolatory topos of observing the return of Nature. This time when June is past, the fading rose finds renewal in the lady's beauty; the "golden Atomes of the day" become "powders to inrich your haire"; the nightingale, when May is past, sings still from within the speaker's lady; the stars when they pass from view find their sphere in her eyes; the phoenix builds in her bosom. Instead of the human taking solace in the renewal of grass and flowers with the spring, Nature is "completed" by Carew's lady. His poetry, as he has often promised, immortalizes her, but in a quite unexpected way. None of the images is new, and yet the effect is that no one has put them together in a more nearly perfect fashion.

A similar commendation through enumeration is to be found in "The Complement" (99 - 101), but the overall effect is altered by wit. Knowing that women no longer believe in the oaths men swear, the speaker must nonetheless swear his love. Accordingly, the first nine stanzas perform a Petrarchan blazon of his beloved under the guise of "swearing" that he does not love her for her eyes; "for that faire, / Rich fanne of thy most curious haire" (ll. 7 - 8); for her cheeks; for her lips or "teeth of pearle" (l. 21); for her neck (described in images from the Song of Songs[11]); for her "mountaines" (l. 31); for her "belly" ("Sleeke as satten, soft as jelly," l. 38); for her thighs ("Happy are those eyes have seene them, / More happy they that saile betweene them," ll. 47 - 48); for her moist palm (thinking, no doubt, as Iago and Othello did, of the sexuality it denotes!), leg, and foot; nor, alas, for her wit (ll. 55 - 60). His own wit, having displayed it throughout as well as in the old pun on "die" as sexual climax (l. 60), he apparently does love.

Now, however, with one of those curious and effective twists by Carew, the ending, as Robin Skelton has suggested, becomes "tender":[12]

> I love not for those eyes, nor haire,
> Nor cheekes, nor lips, nor teeth so rare;
> Nor for thy speech, thy necke, nor breast,
> Nor for thy belly, nor the rest:
> Nor for thy hand, nor foote so small,
> But wouldst thou know (deere sweet) for all.
>
> (ll. 61 - 66)

With a shock, one realizes that Carew has simply employed the rhetorical device of the distribution of arguments followed by a recapitulation. Perhaps as a result of this merging of sentiment with a formal pattern and with metrical ingenuity (six-line stanzas that, in couplets, still experiment with the tetrameters through truncation and catalexis), Carew seems very much at ease in a golden moment of love.

The combination of wit and tenderness in "On a Damaske rose sticking upon a Ladies breast" (108) derives partially from the tradition behind it.[13] The groundwork for complimenting the lady comes through the poet's imagining what glories the rose will know from its vantage point. As in "The Complement," Carew draws upon the Song of Songs for some of his images:

> O happy thou that in that garden rest's,
> That Paradice betweene that Ladies breasts.
> There's an eternall spring; there shalt thou lie,
> Betwixt two lilly mounts, and never die.
> There shalt thou spring amongst the fertile valleyes,
> By budds like thee that grow in midst of Allyes.
>
>   (ll. 5 - 10)

Only a god would dare touch the rose, and any monarch would leave his throne for such a place. Thus the poet persuades himself to an imagined metamorphosis: "My selfe to gaine thy blessed seat do vow, / Would be transformd into a rose as thou" (ll. 21 - 22).

Generally, Carew has borrowed without transforming and reinvigorating the materials borrowed. Also, the principal conception of the poem is merely clever; and the pentameter couplets are more laborious than lucid.

Another familiar genre is tapped in "To the Painter" (106 - 107), in tetrameter couplets, as the poet, following Desportes, is barely willing to admit the possibility that the artist can capture *her* eyes or the red and white of her cheeks, much less that he can ever paint her "virtue." "Besides" (l. 31), a word that conveys the easy conversational tone of the poem, if he succeeds in painting only her outside, he will "teach us superstition" (l. 36), introduce a new saint, "And turne each wandring looker on, / Into a new *Pigmaleon*" (ll. 41 - 42). The clever merging of the "religion of love" with Classical myth then is capped by another conceit, recalling "Celia bleeding, to the Surgeon" (26). Once again the ";mystique knot" formed by the lovers is stressed (ll. 43 - 52).[14]

One of Carew's most unusual poems, "To a Friend" (130), rounds out this group of commendations by sadly commemorating another parting. The first two of the pentameter couplets establish the analogy: one's hand, playing the same "lesson long," establishes a custom; just so, the poet's thoughts, running on this object of his affection for such a long time, cannot yield to other thoughts. The last lines then restate with a new simplicity and naturalness and no coy gallantry Carew's Donnean assertion that only bodies, not minds, are separated when love is true.

The poem recalls the bemused, philosophical tone of "A married Woman" (115 - 16). Except for the references to "passion" (l. 6) and "embraces" (l. 14), indeed, one could accept this as a dissertation on friendship rather than on man-woman love. Carew may simply be platonizing physical love. However, this is one of those poems by him that seem, despite the employment of an analogy, not to have been entirely thought through.

B.   The "Cruell Faire"

Petrarch, Desportes, Ronsard, and others are discernible behind the beautiful poem, "The Spring" (3), but they serve primarily as foils to Carew's own powers.[15] No other poem so well displays his ability to capture a complete mood or picture on a miniature canvas. The pentameter couplets, sometimes tedious in Carew's hands, combine formality and naturalness as they reveal winter (whose frost "Candies the grasse, or castes an ycie creame / Upon the silver Lake," ll. 3 - 4) and the triumphal procession of spring, but, simultaneously, a "drowzie Cuckow" (l. 8), "smiles" and "lowres" (l. 13), and the domestic ox (ll. 17 - 19). The usually remote pastoral figures, Amyntas and Cloris, are caught napping—under a sycamore tree. The spirits of the *reverdie* (the re-greening celebrated in the opening of Chaucer's *Prologue to the Canterbury Tales*) and of the English countryside of Robert Herrick's poems are both present—all as a contrast to the disdainful lady, who is thus subtly charged with being "against Nature." She is still "marble yce" (l. 15) and so "wintry." But *now*, as the poem stresses, is spring, and she is out of step. Already, part of her (the eyes), it is implied, "sees the light" ("*June* in her eyes"). Decorously, the poet bargains sexually too as he points out not only that pastoral lovers "greet the Spring," but that generally love "no more is made / By the fire side" (ll. 19 - 20). This poem is perhaps Carew's most beautiful and most subtle "persuasion to love."

Another classically beautiful poem declaiming against the cold lady is "Red, and white Roses" (46 - 47), also persuasive and argumentative in tone, derivative in its theme (from Joannes Bonefonius and Giambattista Marino), and Herricklike in its delicacy, use of flower-lore, and tetrameter couplets. The white and red roses are emblematic or symbolic of the suffering and innocence of the pleader and of his passion and martyrdom, respectively (ll. 1 - 12). The imperative of the opening ("Reade in these Roses, the sad story / Of my hard fate, and your owne glory") is tempered by the plangency at the last, where there is a shift to pentameter by the addition of catalectic feet: "Oh let your smiles but cleare the weather, / And then they both shall grow together." Rather ingeniously, Carew again suggests that the lady is somehow causing an "unnatural" divorce in Nature by withholding herself from him! She may also be shocked by the fact that the red and white roses, standardly referring to the colors of the lady's complexion, are here transferred to him.

Not so felicitous of execution is "A Song" (105), with the refrain, "Come then and kill me with thy eye, / For if thou let me live, I die," attesting to its conventional language of paradox and its use of the standard pun on "die." The lady's cheeks, lips, and breasts (in successive eight-line stanzas of tetrameter couplets) revive him from the death wrought by her disdain. A single example, labeled by one critic "perhaps the most improbable figure Carew ever concocted,"[16] will suffice:

> In her faire cheekes two pits doe lye,
> To bury those slaine by her eye,
> So spight of death this comforts me,
> That fairely buried I shall be.
> My grave with rose and lilly spread,
> O 'tis a life to be so dead.
> > Come then and kill me with thy eye,
> > For if thou let me live, I die.
> > > (ll. 1 - 8)

With such "antidotes" always available, only one alternative remains for the lady: "Your way's to bury me alive / In Cupids cave" (ll. 30 - 31). The sense of resolution is emphasized by the fact that the final stanza is extended to ten lines.

The basic idea for "A Prayer to the Wind" (11 - 12) comes from Petrarch, and Carew's version was put to music by Henry Lawes.

The poet tells the "gentle whispering wind" to be his emissary to the reluctant lady. The lover's sigh to be delivered by this go-between will be cast at her breast and "set her heart afire" (l. 6). The poet then imagines the wind's journey over her body in a short and generalized blazon (ll. 7 - 18). Invigorated by this experience, the wind on its return can change "Every weed into a flower" (l. 20). The lover, thinking of the wind's power, adds a final request, sensing that he will have a friend through this encounter with his mistress:

> Thou canst with thy powerfull blast,
> Heat apace, and coole as fast:
> Thou canst kindle hidden flame,
> And ag'en destroy the same;
> Then for pittie, either stir
> Up the fire of love in her,
> That alike both flames may shine,
> Or else quite extinguish mine.
>   (ll. 25 - 32)[17]

Once again, the lover asks for mutual love or no love at all.

Despite the fact that many manuscript versions of this poem exist, it still is not among Carew's more successful productions. The stratagem of the conceit remains uppermost. The tetrameter couplets are engaging, however, for the use of truncated feet.

The theme of the "cruell faire" is also treated in "On sight of a Gentlewomans face in the water" (102), which is in quatrains (abab) and alternates tetrameter and trimeter lines. The "floods" are told to be still (biblical parody?) and not deface her image, thereby acquiring for themselves "Votaries from every place" (l. 3). Quickly they must congeal the reflection to crystal in order to mirror the inner truth about the lady: "How cold, how hard she is" (l. 12). Thus far, the poem is quite typical in its own "reflection" of some of the poet's favored images (e.g., congealing, crystallizing). Now Carew typifies his style by an "original" ending:

> But if the envious *Nymphes* shall feare,
>   Their beauties will be scorn'd,
> And hire the ruder winds to teare
>   That face which you adorn'd,

> Then rage and foame amaine that we
>   Their malice may despise:
> When from your froath we soone shall see,
>   A second *Venus* rise.
> (ll. 13 - 20).

Criticism of the disdainful woman has been turned to compliment
that encourages her to think of the two of them as a unit
("we / Their malice may despise") against jealous women. While
the lover shows her how necessary he is to her "safety," he romps
outrageously with the compliment of Classical allusion.

The "disdains" of the lady gradually bring on a declaration of
leaving her in the pentameter couplets of "Song. Murdring
beautie" (8). It again exploits both the oxymora of love from the
sonnet tradition and the old Renaissance pun on "die." The
"calmes and tempests of her smiles and frownes" (l. 4) work him
equal harm. Only in relinquishment is there hope:

> I'le love no more those cruell eyes of hers,
> Which pleas'd or anger'd still are murderers:
> For if she dart (like lightning) through the ayre
> Her beames of wrath, she kils me with despaire.
> If shee behold me with a pleasing eye,
> I surfet with excesse of joy, and dye.
> (ll. 5 - 10)

Little originality is to be found in this specimen, except in the supposed resolution to be done with the lady.

Apparently, the poet-lover can think better of such a pledge,
however, and tries one more ploy—"Truce in Love entreated" (41).
The armistice he attempts to effect is with Cupid, "the blind God":

> . . . for see my heart
> Is made thy Quiver, where remaines
> No voyd place for another Dart. . . .
> (ll. 1 - 3)

Besides, he is such "tame and unresisting prey" (l. 6) that he cannot
be much sport. Cleverly, he entices Cupid to stalk a "nobler foe,"
his disdainful lady: "If thou dar'st equall combat try, / Wound her,
for 'tis for her I dye" (ll. 11 - 12). Indebted as it is to Ovid,
Desportes, and others, the poem is still a pleasing trifle in its two

six-line tetrameter stanzas (ababcc).

Having run out of expedients to sail him along the course of love, the speaker in the dialogue, "A Lover upon an Accident necessitating his departure, consults with Reason" (48), seeks outside help:

> *Fortune* destroys me if I stay,
> *Love* kills me if I goe away:
> Since *Love*, and *Fortune*, both are blind,
> Come *Reason*, and resolve my doubtfull mind.
>   (ll. 5 - 8)

Reason urges him to forsake "the blinder God" (l. 10) and let "Blind *Fortune*" be his guide (l. 9), "For, my just hand may sometime move / The wheele of *Fortune*, not the spheare of *Love*" (ll. 15 - 16). Other poems show that the lesson does not "take," but the chat with Reason is a refreshing change of pace from the poet's customary erotic obsessions. Carew probably enjoyed the incongruity between the pretentious title and the slender poem (two tetrameter stanzas, rhyming ababccdd, and with the last line of each shifting to pentameter).

C.   *Rules of Courtship*

As in the case of the love poems to Celia and to his mistress, this group on the general theme of love and courtship contains declarations of the expectations and demands of the participants; e.g., secrecy, eternal devotion. So the lover in "Song. Eternitie of love protested" (23 - 24) yields to the pressures of the game of love as prescribed by Petrarchanism when he distinguishes his "true flame" from the "pale weake" one of lesser lovers, whose heat, "like paper set on fire, / Burne[s], and expire[s]!" (ll. 5 - 6). His will endure beyond the grave and "shall waite on me to the lower shade" (l. 13). Once again, "True love can never change his seat, / Nor did he ever love, that could retreat" (ll. 7 - 8). The only parts of this exercise meriting special attention are the image of the lover's "flame" (a separate entity waiting for him on the other side of death) and the variation of the couplets from pentameter to dimeter to tetrameter.

The lover-speaker is just as certain that he will not break the code of secrecy as he uses Catullus, Donne,[18] and others to state his commitment in "Secresie protested" (11). Portions of Carew's own "Celia bleeding, to the Surgeon" (26) and "To the Painter" (106 -

107) are called to mind as well in the last conceit of the poem:

> This only meanes may find it out,
> If when I dye, Physicians doubt
> What caus'd my death, and there to view
> Of all their judgements which was true,
> Rip up my heart, Oh then I feare
> The world will see thy picture there.
> (ll. 11 - 16)

The reader would expect the argument to run that, so long as no outsider knows of their love, nothing is wrong with loving. No such cynicism creeps in here, as the need for secrecy presses from the "hallowedness" and "preciousness" of their love through the finely woven wit of the last and through the singing tetrameter couplets.

So ardent a lover must certainly have a convincing "An Excuse of absence" (131); in fact it is the same Carew adapted from Donne for "To *Celia*, upon Love's Ubiquity" (123 - 24). If only for its kinship with "A Valediction: Forbidding Mourning,"[19] the poem is worth quoting in full:

> You'le aske perhaps wherefore I stay,
> Loving so much, so long away,
> O doe not thinke t'was I did part,
> It was my body, not my hearte,
> For like a Compasse in your love,   5
> One foote is fix'd and cannot moove,
> The other may follow her blinde guide
> Of giddy fortune, but not slide
> Beyound your service, nor dares venture
> To wander farre from you the Center.   10

Carew's poem lacks the beauty of Donne's compass image, yet it should be noticed for the emotion of ll. 3 - 4 and for the introduction of a practical sway on any man, with the effective turn Carew gives to the "blinde guide / Of giddy fortune." The overall failure is strange. Carew is better at adopting Donne's style of reasoning, conversational discourse than he is here at lifting a single image. Yet very often his forte seems to be the extended analysis of a single image. Almost as if he felt his failure, he has had difficulty too with the tetrameter couplets. His catalectic lines are ordinarily apt; but, for example, ll. 7, 9, and 10 of this poem are discordant.

If these three poems, "Eternitie of love protested," "Secresie protested," and "An Excuse of absence," represent the demands and expectations of the lady, the lover also imposes or tries to impose certain conditions. Philosophical means[20] and extremes, another example of Carew's Metaphysical yoking of the abstruse with matters of love, are played upon in "Mediocritie in love rejected" (12 - 13), in tetrameters and with an unusual rhyme scheme, one of his most popular and yet conventional poems. It is used by one critic to represent Carew's most common structure,[21] but the presence of an identical opening and closing line is a novelty. Also worth noting is the Classical mythology (Danaë and perhaps the Promethean overtones of "Vulture-hopes" in l.11) to prove the general position that "Either extreame, of love, or hate, / Is sweeter than a calme estate" (ll. 5 - 6). Again, one is impressed, despite the indebtedness, with the production, especially with the combination of a rejection of the Classical mean (unusual in Carew's period) and a play on the alternate burning and freezing of the unrequited lover of sonnet fame.[22]

D. *The Lady's Point of View*

Often in Carew's poetry, as would be expected from a poet steeped in the sonnet tradition, the woman stands accused of crimes against love in general and against the lover in particular. But occasionally Carew, in company with the Italian poet, Torquato Tasso and others, allows her to litigate, as in "In the person of a Lady to her inconstant servant" (40). The lady devotes the first two stanzas to recalling the past glories of their courtship when her lover wooed with all the accepted paraphernalia of the "religion of love" (the "Altar" of her hand, "an humble Martyr," an oath by her eyes). She, it is recorded, responded to save him from "death" and in the second stanza testifies to her poor return: "My soule enflam'd with thy false breath, / Poyson'd with kisses, suckt in death" (ll. 13 - 14). The last stanza, however, flashes with the wit that is usually the especial province of the male:

> Yet I nor hand, nor lip will more,
>> Revenge, or mercy, to procure
> From the offended God of love;
>> My curse is fatall, and my pure
>> Love, shall beyond thy scorne endure:
> If I implore the Gods, they'le find
> Thee too ingratefull, me too kind.
>> (ll. 15 - 21)

She cannot curse without destroying him for whom her love would
persist even beyond the merciful attempts by the gods to obliterate
it—a new consideration of the old belief in proving love by suffering for it! One can only wish that there were a little less regularity
in the prosody (three seven-line tetrameter stanzas, rhyming
ababbcc) to support her charges of his inconstancy.

"A Ladies prayer to Cupid" (131), translated from Guarini's
"Madrigal CIX" and in pentameter couplets, probably belongs to
the period Carew spent in Italy in the service of Sir Dudley
Carleton. It is a different and pleasing glimpse of the female, at
once psychologically apt and witty. She wants not a "fond boy or
page" but a *man*, unforgettably capping her description of him with
"Let him within / Weare all his beard, and none uppon his chinn"
(l. 10). Carew has captured for the female the same zest in the game
of love that characterizes the male speaker of "The second Rapture" (103 - 104), who looks forward to the felicity of having "a
wench about thirteene."

Three other attempts to catch the female's point of view are
found in Carew's poetry, though in none of these does she assert her
own voice. In "To A. L. Perswasions to love" (4 - 6), discussed in
Chapter 5, one of the major "persuasions" is the pleasure *she* will
feel:

> Did the thing for which I sue
> Onely concerne my selfe not you,
> Were men so fram'd as they alone
> Reap'd all the pleasure, women none,
> Then had you reason to be scant;
> But 'twere a madnesse not to grant
> That which affords (if you consent)
> To you the giver, more content
> Then me the beggar. . . .
> (ll. 17 - 25)

The last two, both entitled "Good counsel to a young Maid" (13,
25), are quite different in tone from either "To A. L. Perswasions to
Love," "A Ladies prayer to Cupid," or "The Second Rapture."
While they speak the same language of warning against being taken
in by the speaker or by other men, they are also quite different from
each other.

The first, in iambic tetrameter tercets (aaa) with truncated lines,
is both dainty and original in the new twist it gives to the old im-

ages of the mirror and the blush. The false mirror is the tears from
the cunning lover's eyes and the "nets" of cunning poetry. Her own
blushes are her best safeguard and weave through the poem from
the second stanza to the climactic last line with its controlled horror
of the "perpetuall blush." A shamming by the pining and pale unrequited lover, Carew suggests, has tricked many a lady (notably
the one in his own "In the person of a Lady to her inconstant servant"); so, too, have poems. To underscore his point, he makes that
last stanza proverbial, as he already had l. 6 ("Beautie takes a foyle
from woe").

The daintiness of the stanzas, each with its homogeneous rhymes,
appropriate for the addressee, stands in functional contrast to the
promised woes should the advice fail to be heeded. The "Tender
Maid" is educated in the ways of the world by the juxtaposition of
poems and their attempts to "catch thy maiden-head." Worse is
Stanza 5 with its double meaning. If she takes pity with her
"melting heart" and "cures" by requiting, she will get for her
reward not only an equal passion (the burning "calenture," an image used frequently by Donne and Carew), which will soon burn
hopelessly when the lover has had his fill of her, but perhaps a real
"Loves disease," from the male version of which Carew himself was
thought to suffer.

The second "Good counsell to a young Maid" (25) draws an extended water analogy, but the streams from the eyes this time are
Hers—and they will not be sham ones. For the analogy, Carew uses
the standard motif of the lover as pilgrim (as employed, for example, by Shakespeare in the meeting of Romeo and Juliet); but his
object of pilgrimage is not the lady as shrine but as nymph of the
"watering-place" along the route. Therein is the cue: once the lover
has quelled his thirst, he will be on to the next stop or his new conquest. In addition to inverting the relationships of the water
analogy he has used in "To my Mistris sitting by a Rivers side. An
Eddy" (14), Carew has "converted" the religious imagery applied
to secular love to read the maiden a lesson not in the high devotion
of the lover but in the rules of the chase. Alike in theme but very
different in approach from its sister-poem, it too is a masterful piece
of poetry. Its three six-line stanzas (ababcc), mixing pentameter and
tetrameter lines, move smoothly and unerringly to the lesson.

E.   *General Thoughts on Love*

The poet has thoughts about a different species of female, the
woman he would marry, in "A married Woman" (115 - 16), one of

the oddest and most difficult of his poems.[23] If his wife is not already "thus moulded," he will "create this mind" (1. 2): she must obey him as the flesh must be taught to obey the soul; the appetite, the reason. The syntax of the next couplets is difficult; if obedience becomes an habitual virtue, the result is a calmness of temperament (and of marriage) that allows no such passions as lust and anger. Bearing out the analogy of ll. 7 - 8, the speaker now generalizes from his wife being obedient to him to the lower faculties being obedient to the higher ones. If anger, then, leads a man to murder, or lust leads him to commit adultery, it will not "suffice to say my sense, the Beast/Provokt me to't" (ll. 19 - 20). Only if he could divest himself of his soul and so become a beast were such reasoning good. The connection between Adam and Eve (ll. 23 - 24), used as proof of his line of reasoning, and himself and his imagined wife seems tenuous at best. From the woman's point of view, the main salvation is that, though she must first "learne t'obay," when obedience becomes habitual, "no rough sway / Shall once appeare" (ll. 9 - 10). A small consolation also emerges from the notion that "she perhaps had beene / Unpunisht" (ll. 25 - 26) were it not for the fact that *he* sinned. Carew wittily rewrites the Bible here, but his attempt to capture the tone of a Donnean disquisition results in obscurity and prolixity.

A serious note also maintains itself in the idealistic "Loves Force" (116), which likewise employs pentameter couplets. "In the first ruder Age, when Love was wild" (1. 1), Reason was not in existence; and "So men their undistinguisht females tooke / By chance, not choyce" (ll. 10 - 11). Fortunately, this confusion was brought to order:

> . . . soone the heavenly sparke
> That in mans bosome lurkt, broke through this darke
> Confusion, then the noblest breast first felt
> It selfe, for its owne proper object melt.
> (ll. 11 - 14)[24]

The beautiful thought of these last lines is enhanced by the sudden smoothing of the verse.

Mild cynicism about the love game returns with "Song. Conquest by flight" (15), the novelty being that men *and* women are warned by the obviously experienced poet to "flye betimes, for only they / Conquer love that run away" (ll. 15 - 16). The address to the ladies sounds the themes of the two poems providing "good counsel

to a young maid" and of "In the person of a Lady to her inconstant
servant":

> Ladyes, flye from Love's smooth tale,
> Oathes steep'd in teares doe oft prevaile;
> Griefe is infectious, and the ayre
> Enflam'd with sighes, will blast the fayre:
> Then stop your eares, when lovers cry,
> Lest your selfe weepe, when no soft eye
> Shall with a sorrowing teare repay
> That pittie which you cast away.
>   (ll. 1 - 8)

The advice to the *young* men (Stanza 2) is a less characteristic
Carew excursion. It plays on the contradictions and paradoxes of the
sonnet tradition with its emphasis on conquering by running away.
Clever too are the adaptation of Cupid's darts for the instruments of
the women and the understated theme—"Beware; if the ladies do
not get you one way, they will another (lips or eyes or smile or kiss
. . . every man can be caught)." As if to reinforce the point, the
verse itself is "Love's smooth tale" in tetrameter couplets (with
some truncation).

Carew is more himself in the last two poems of this group. In
"The tinder" (104), he indulges in self-mockery, though this type of
poem was popularized by Ovid, Marino, and others. In trochaic
tetrameter couplets, he wonders what Nature has been about in his
production, for ". . . no woman can come neere me / Faire, but
her I court to heare me" (ll. 3 - 4). His first lady must have "Burnt
in rage my heart to tinder" (l. 7, with a pun on "tender"), and thus
he gives fair warning (and a fair come-on): "Women since you thus
inflame me, / Flint and steele Il'e ever name yee" (ll. 11 -
12)—women will forever make him "tender." Under the pretense
that he is an "easy mark," while ladies remain hard as steel, he has
baited a trap to match that of his literary "son," William
Wycherley's Horner from *The Country Wife*. The wary female is
served notice by the fact that seven of the twelve lines end on *me;*
one ends on *yee*.

As if to outrage his critics further and so reaffirm his reputation
for libertinism, Carew alludes to his earlier "success" in "The second Rapture" (103 - 104), an ironic reworking, in tetrameter
couplets, of the ancient quest for the *summum bonum*. It is not his
pun on *die*, but the age of his chosen mate that has caused some

modern critics to recoil, though in Carew's day, thirteen was still a proper age for young girls to marry. The problem is that he is offensive to some because he obviously is not thinking of marriage and because he sings his couplets so disarmingly:

> No worldling, no, tis not thy gold,
> Which thou dost use but to behold;
> Nor fortune, honour, nor long life,
> Children, or friends, nor a good wife,
> That makes thee happy; these things be
> But shaddowes of felicitie.
> Give me a wench about thirteene,
> Already voted to the Queene
> Of lust and lovers. . . .
>
> (ll. 1 - 9)

Here are all the ingredients of traditional compliment—the blazon with, in particular, a new wording for the fact that his mistress's eyes "outshine the sun" (ll. 17 - 18); Classical allusions to draw implicit acknowledgment that she is a goddess; and a subtle reaffirmation that love is a "religion" as he dismisses the petty desires of "worldlings." Shock is registered not merely from the age of the girl and the fact that she is already devoted "to the Queene / Of lust and lovers," but from the subtle use of biblical overtones in this so sexual a poem—e.g., the hair that "spreads her shoulders like a tent / And is her vaile and ornament" (ll. 11 - 12), the "threescore yeares and longer" (l. 16), and the "lesser lights of skie" (l. 18). In fact, the whole poem can be taken as a parody of the story of David being given a young virgin to warm him in his old age (I Kings, 1:1 - 5).

The reader has to try very hard to remember that Carew can also be tender, almost saccharine at times. Otherwise, Carew is likely to be assessed on the basis of poems like "The second Rapture" as merely a libertine, the reputation from which he has suffered almost until the present time.

CHAPTER 4

Carew as Critic and Contributor

C AREW'S elegy on John Donne is often hailed as a masterpiece of criticism, and his general comments on Ben Jonson also garner praise from critics. Not widely noticed is the fact that the love lyrics too are threaded with comments on poetry and the poet that deserve consideration.

I   Carew on the Poet and Poetry

A.   *The Subject Immortalized by Poetry*

Carew can be simply derivative in his attitudes toward poetry and the task of the poet. He frequently revives, for example, the Renaissance emphasis on poetry as a stay against Time for his "perswasions to love." The last three tercets of "On his Mistres lookeinge in a glasse" (132) argue (1) that his lady should not be disdainful, for his verse has made her known to the world; (2) that if she forsakes her disdain, she will be celebrated as not only fair, but kind; and (3) that his verse can chase away decay and endow her with an "immortal" grace.

Similarly, the ending of "A New-yeares Sacrifice. To Lucinda" (32 - 33) urges the conventional promise of immortality through poetry. It also stresses the need for poetic inspiration:

> So may my Goddesse from her heaven, inspire
> My frozen bosome with a Delphique fire,
> And then the world shall by that glorious flame,
> Behold the blaze of thy immortall name.
> (ll. 23 - 26)

Since the Countess of Carlisle ("Lucinda") was already famous, however, Carew seems to intend more than the conventional here. He has established her in the pentameter couplets of the poem as a goddess, who, thus, should not be prayed *for* (as others do in praying for blessings of the New Year upon her), but prayed *to*, a slight variation on the mistress-as-goddess of Petrarchan love lyrics.

In the four lines quoted, he also seems to woo the Countess, for the "frozen bosome" to be inspired "with a Delphique fire" can refer not only to his "hard-bound" status as a poet, but to the alternation from freezing (the result of disdain) to burning (lust) of the sonnet lover. The lady may choose to ignore the latter interpretation as perfunctory court gallantry, and the invitation will be forgotten. Nonetheless, the conventional role of poet and poetry is employed for a precise purpose.

In "Ingratefull beauty threatned" (17 - 18), Carew warns that he will withdraw Celia's fame and immortality by ceasing to write poems about her, for she apparently is not obeying the rules of their relationship. His verse saved her from the fate of the "forgotten crowd" and "exhal'd" her name (ll. 3 - 5). Her "killing power" is all his, the poet's: "Thou art my starre, shin'st in my skies" (l. 10). Fools may adore her "mystique formes," but he created them and can "uncreate": "Wise Poets that wrap't Truth in tales, / Knew her themselves, through all her vailes" (ll. 17 - 18). The originality of the poem comes not from its materials but from their use; he does not plead and persuade but bluntly unfolds his blackmail. If poetry is to remain all powerful, as it has already shown what it can do, so now it must show what it can "undo." The specific use of the powers of poetry is Carew's own, but the recognition of its powers echoes Renaissance poetry and Renaissance poetic theorists, especially Sidney.

In "Griefe ingrost" (44 - 45), the common sense of the speaker rebukes him for his "sad numbers . . . / So full of woe" (ll. 1 - 2), suggesting that revenge against his disdainful lady is easily attained:

> If she must still denie,
> Weepe not, but dye:
> And in thy Funerall fire,
> Shall all her fame expire.
> Thus both shall perish, and as thou on thy Hearse
> Shall want her teares, so she shall want thy Verse;
> Repine not then at thy blest state:
> Thou art above thy fate. . . .
> (ll. 5 - 12)

While the comments on poetry and its powers are justified, the extremity of the remedy proffered converts the poem into a gentle self-laughter even as the lover pretends quite seriously to await Celia's pronouncement of his own doom.

The lady herself is convinced of immortality through poetry in "A Pastorall Dialogue" (42 - 44):

> . . . I
> Shall live in thy immortall rime,
> Untill the Muses dye.
> (ll. 46 - 48)

Whether it comes from the lady, however, or, as is the more customary, from the poet-lover, the conventional theme of immortality through poetry is persistent enough to suggest a more than conventional concern, on Carew's part, with the poet and his craft.

B. *True and Serious Poetry*

Two poems proclaim that only *true* poetry can perform such service for love as immortalizing the mistress. The would-be wooer in "Boldnesse in love" (42) is advised not simply to be "bold" but, indirectly at least, to produce *moving accents:*

> But when with moving accents, thou
> Shalt constant faith, and service vow,
> Thy *Celia* shall receive those charmes
> With open eares, and with unfolded armes.
> (ll. 13 - 16)

Implicit here is the condemnation of the "poet-mongers" who evoked such righteous indignation from Ben Jonson. Anyone can praise a mistress in "whining poetry," and any woman can fall for it. The true poet and the true woman so complimented seek their own levels. Thus "To my Rivall" (41) likewise implies that poor poetry may "incline" looser women, but that Celia

> . . . must have offerings more divine;
> Such pearlie drops, as youthfull *May*
> Scatters before the rising day;
> Such smooth soft language, as each line
> Might stroake an angry God, or stay
> *Joves* thunder, make the hearers pine
> With envie; doe this, thou shalt be
> Servant to her, Rivall with me.
> (ll. 7 - 14)

Interestingly, Carew's description of the "smooth soft language" of the good love poet could easily apply to the works on love for which he is now most famous. The joke is on the rival, who surely has no idea that he must rival not only as lover but as poet.

Carew's seriousness about the craft of poetry is also conveyed incidentally in the not-very-serious "To T. H. a Lady resembling my Mistresse" (26 - 27). Enticing "T. H." to a casual affair, he suggests the rigors of "art":

> Disdaine not a divided heart,
> Though all be hers, you shall have part;
> Love is not tyde to rules of art.
> (ll. 4 - 6)

Elsewhere, Carew implies that the woman wooed by the poet must herself be a critic capable of distinguishing true from false verse. "Good counsel to a young Maid" (13) rather cynically observes:

> Netts, of passions finest thred,
> Snaring Poems, will be spred,
> All, to catch thy maiden-head.
> (ll. 10 - 12)

In "To a Lady that desired I would love her" (81 - 82), the speaker pleads for mutual love.[1] If she refuses to yield to his pure love, she will give rise to myriads of poor "Petrarchan" lovers bemoaning their unrequited agonies. Their poems with such Petrarchan conceits of *wounds, flames,* and *darts* cannot do justice to her charms. His verse, on the other hand, will use all of "Rich Natures store" (l. 31), the true source of poetry, to commend her if she responds in equal love—

> Then give me leave to love, and love me too,
>   Not with designe
> To rayse, as Loves curst Rebells doe,
>   When puling Poets whine,
> Fame to their beautie, from their blubbr'd eyne.
>
> Griefe is a puddle, and reflects not cleare
>   Your beauties rayes,
> Joyes are pure streames, your eyes appeare
>   Sullen in sadder layes,
> In chearfull numbers they shine bright with prayse;

> Which shall not mention to expresse you fayre
>   Wounds, flames, and darts,
>   Stormes in your brow, nets in your haire,
>   Suborning all your parts,
> Or to betray, or torture captive hearts.
>   (ll. 11 - 25)

In this poem, considered structurally among his best,[2] Carew
could be defining the two major classes of his own love poetry: that
which remains steadfastly within chosen conventions, usually
Petrarchan, with only occasional flights; and that which is his own
distinctive voice in love—mirrored in the naturalness and seeming
artlessness of Stanza 6 of "To a Lady that desired I would love her":

> I'le make your eyes like morning Suns appeare,
>   As milde, and faire;
>   Your brow as Crystall smooth, and cleare,
>   And your dishevell'd hayre
> Shall flow like a calme Region of the Ayre.

Nothing, it is true, is new in this passage. How many times has one
heard of "eyes like morning Suns"? How many times has Carew
himself used "crystal" to describe the lady? The image of the
"dishevell'd hayre" echoes many seventeenth-century poets,
notably Jonson, but what of the disheveled hair flowing "like a
calme Region of the Ayre"? That last and the whole stanza
miraculously and "uncannily" become his own. And even the
"conventional" poetry surpasses that of those "puling Poets" he
distinguishes from himself. The theory behind the "true" poetry is
always there if he sometimes lacks the staying power to activate it.
   The slight, rather strange little poem, "A Fancy" (117), also
makes a strong case for the worthwhileness of poetry beyond its
mere surface texture. The meeting of the poet's paper and pen is
likened to that of ladies and their makeup, which not only serves
cosmetic purposes but speaks "To the skild Lover, and
relate[s] / Unheard, his sad or happy Fate" (ll. 11 - 12). This
analogy may be unfortunate, but the description of the operation of
a true poem is apt:

> Nor doe their Characters delight,
> As carelesse workes of black and white:
> But 'cause you underneath may find
> A sence that can enforme the mind;

> Divine, or moral rules impart
> Or Raptures of Poetick Art:
> So what at first was only fit
> To fold up silkes, may wrap up wit.
> (ll. 13 - 20)

As in the case of the proper audience for the love poem, that is, *Celia*, not "looser" women, so here there seems to be a lurking feeling that not all will be able to find "underneath" "A sence that can enforme the mind"—the slightest tinge of the Miltonic "fit audience find, though few."

Carew also emphasizes the versatility of good poetry. At the end of "To the Countesse of Anglesie upon the immoderatly-by-her-lamented death of her Husband" (69 - 71), he hopes to turn from elegy to commendation of the lady, thereby subtly promising her recovery from grief as he attests to the rich possibilities of verse:

> Then let him rest joyn'd to great *Buckingham*,
> And with his brothers, mingle his bright flame:
> Looke up, and meet their beames, and you from thence
> May chance derive a chearfull influence.
> Seeke him no more in dust, but call agen
> Your scatterd beauties home, and so the pen
> Which now I take from this sad Elegie
> Shall sing the Trophies of your conquering eye.
> (ll. 79 - 86)

A less solemn stress on the versatility of good poetry is set forth in "To the New-yeare, for the Countesse of Carlile" (91 - 92). Carew intimates here that if he finds grace with "Lucinda" and she thinks this poem is worthy, she must wait until next year to see how good a poem can really be:

> *Janus*, if when next I trace
> Those sweet lines, I in her face
> Reade the Charter of my grace,
>
> Then from bright *Apollo's* tree,
> Such a Garland wreath'd shall be,
> As shall Crowne both Her and thee.
> (ll. 19 - 24)

Janus is playfully "blackmailed" into throwing his weight on the side of the poet and getting poetic plaudits in return. So powerful is poetry that the very gods want to be celebrated in it! And Carew gets to exercise his wit in adapting the god of poetry and the poetic garland to his contextual needs. The tercets themselves anticipate the poetic garland promised.

Even when Carew is being playful and wittily flippant, however, his belief in the heightened state of poetry is evident. For example, in "My mistris commanding me to returne her letters" (9 - 11), he tells the letters:

> Though these be powerfull arguments to prove
> I love in vaine; yet I must ever love.
> Say, if she frowne when you that word rehearse,
> Service in prose, is oft call'd love in verse:
> Then pray her, since I send back on my part
> Her papers, she will send me back my heart.
>   (ll. 25 - 30)

In "On the Duke of *Buckingham*" (57), he carefully distinguishes verse and chronicle:

> His Actions let our Annals tell:
> Wee write no Chronicle; This Pile
> Weares onely sorrowes face and stile,
> Which, even the envie that did waite
> Upon his flourishing estate,
> Turn'd to soft pitty of his death,
> Now payes his Hearse; but that cheape breath
> Shall not blow here, nor th' unpure brine
> Puddle those streames that bathe this shrine.
>   (ll. 16 - 24)

This contrast between chronicle and poetry, with the higher claim being made for the latter, is reminiscent of both Donne's "The Canonization"—

> And if unfit for tombes and hearse
> Our legend bee, it will be fit for verse;
> And if no peece of Chronicle wee prove,
>   We'll build in sonnets pretty roomes. . . .
>   (ll. 29 - 32)

—and his "The First Anniversary," where he speaks of the reasons for his *verse* treatment of Elizabeth Drury—

> . . . if you
> In reverence to her, do thinke it due,
> That no one should her praises thus rehearse,
> As matter fit for Chronicle, not verse;
> Vouchsafe to call to minde that God did make
> A last, and lasting'st peece, a song. He spake
> To *Moses* to deliver unto all,
> That song, because hee knew they would let fall
> The Law, the Prophets, and the History,
> But keepe the song still in their memory. . . .

> . . .

> Verse hath a middle nature: heaven keepes Soules,
> The Grave keepes bodies, Verse the Fame enroules.
> (ll. 457 - 66, 473 - 74)[3]

While it seems likely that Carew is following Donne in such distinctions between verse and "chronicle," one cannot overlook what at least on the surface is a contradiction of this elevation of poetry. Gustavus Adolphus appears to be matter fit for chronicle, not verse; in "In answer of an Elegiacall Letter Upon the death of the King of Sweden from Aurelian Townsend, inviting me to write on that subject" (74 - 77), Carew refuses the task proposed by his friend:

> *Virgil,* nor *Lucan,* no, nor *Tasso* more
> Then both, not *Donne,* worth all that went before,
> With the united labour of their wit
> Could a just Poem to this subject fit,
> His actions were too mighty to be rais'd
> Higher by Verse, let him in prose be prays'd,
> In modest faithfull story, which his deedes
> Shall turne to Poems. . . .
> (ll. 11 - 18)

The highest compliment Carew can pay is not to write a poem on the dead King of Sweden, whose deeds were too "mighty to be rais'd / Higher by Verse." If he is praised in "prose," "In modest faithfull story," his deeds will turn these records into poems anyway. For one reason, the acts of Gustavus Adolphus, however simply stated, will seem so preposterous as to suggest the "feigning" associated with poetry from the time of Plato. Such a "Caesar" must be left to annals and journals, where each of his days may be cut into minutes, a feat impossible for the compact, distilled poem. Only by the prosaic recording of each "minute's" activities can the world be expected to believe the claims made for this man of war. Beyond that, all must be left to Providence; and the English, in particular, Carew records in the remainder of his poem, must take a different way in politics and in poetry (a way discussed in the upcoming section on Carew's comments about his own poetry). The turning from verse to prose here is for the immediate purpose of compliment, as it removes the possible label of insult from Carew's refusal to commemorate the dead king in a poem; he has, moreover, under the guise of refusing the task, provided a commendatory elegy in the first place. By this "refusal," he has also given himself an opportunity to define what he feels to be the distinctive British Muse.

"Upon Master W. Mountague his returne from travell" (77 - 78) lays special emphasis on the ties among all poets. On the one hand, the returning Montagu "deals his *body*" among his friends, while from his fellow poet, Carew,

> . . . my glad soule sends
> This her embrace: Thus we of *Delphos* greet,
> As Lay-men claspe their hands, we joyne our [poetic] feet.
> (ll. 38 - 40)

At the same time, the versatility of poetry is again revealed, for the whole poem salutes the return of his friend, while the "poem-within-the-poem"[4] (ll. 13 - 36) forms an actual blessing by the "Muses Quire" of the "fayre Gale that drove his ship to land" (ll. 11 - 12):

> Sweetly breathing Vernall Ayre,
> That with kind warmth doest repayre
> Winters ruines, from whose brest
> All the gums, and spice of th' East
> Borrow their perfumes, whose eye
> Guilds the morne, and cleares the skie,
> Whose disheveld tresses shed
> Pearles upon the Violet bed,
> On whose brow with calme smiles drest
> The Halcion sits and builds her nest:
> Beautie, Youth, and endlesse spring,
> Dwell upon thy rosie wing.
> Thou, if stormie Boreas throwes
> Downe whole Forrests when he blowes,

> With a pregnant flowery birth
> Canst refresh the teeming Earth;
> If he nip the early bud,
> If he blast what's faire or good;
> If he scatter our choyce flowers,
> If he shake our hills or bowers,
> If his rude breath threaten us,
> Thou canst stroake great AEolus,
> And from him the grace obtaine,
> To binde him in an Iron chaine.[5]

The discursive pentameter couplets of the main poem embed the incantation formed by the tetrameters.

While his moods can vary, generally, then, Carew takes the poet's craft very seriously and believes in the powers of its product. As he subscribes to the standard Renaissance theme of the antipathy between Nature and the artificiality of art, as in "Upon a Ribband" (29), where the "silken wreath" is the product of art, while "Nature fram'd" the love it symbolizes (l. 21),[6] one does not forget that he has elsewhere defined "Rich Natures store" as "the Poets Treasure" ("To a Lady that desired I would love her," l. 31).

Moreover, among his nine paraphrases of the Psalms, he has chosen two which could be turned to the task of the poet. Verses 1 and 32 - 35 of the enumerative Psalm 104 (139 - 42) are thus translated by Carew:

> My soule the great Gods prayses sings,
> Encircled round with gloryes wings. . . .
>
> . . .
>
> The stedfast Earth shall shake, if hee
> Look downe, & if the Mountaines bee
> Toucht, they shall smoak. Yet still my verse
> Shall whilst I live his praise reherse;
>
> In him with joy my thoughts shall meete,
> Hee makes my Meditations sweete.
>
> The Sinner shall appeare noe more.
> Then oh my Soule, thy Lord adore.

Verses 13 - 16 of Psalm 119 (144 - 49) receive this paraphrasing:

> I have publisht the divine
> Judgments of thy Mouth with myne,
>
> Which have filld my Soule with pleasure
> More then all the heaps of treasure.
>
> They shall all the Subject prove
> Of my talk, and of my love;
>
> Those my darlings noe tyme shall
> From my Memory lett fall.

At a task, paraphrasing the Psalms, that most critics have felt Carew to be little concerned about, he nevertheless chooses "songs" relevant to his own work as poet. Usually considered a kind of apprentice work, the nine Psalms may be his attempt to sort out or find his own thoughts on the possibilities of poetry and its meters. There are five-line tetrameter stanzas (ababb) in numbers 1, 2, 91, 113, 114, and 137; tetrameter stanzas of a varying number of lines in 51 and 104; and tetrameter couplet stanzas in 119.

C. *Carew's Comments on His Own Poetry*

The poem "To my worthy friend Master Geo. Sand[y]s, on his translation of the Psalmes" (93 - 94) has promoted the tradition that Carew underwent a conversion in his last years. Among the few poems published during his life, it first appeared in 1638, in the second edition of Sandys's *A Paraphrase upon the Divine Poems*. In it, Carew exposes his secular Muse:

> I Presse not to the Quire, nor dare I greet
> The holy place with my unhallowed feet;
> My unwasht Muse, polutes not things Divine,
> Nor mingles her prophaner notes with thine;
> Here, humbly at the porch she listning stayes,
> And with glad eares sucks in thy sacred layes.
>   (ll. 1 - 6)

As penitents of old were allowed to hear the liturgies if not to assist in the church services, so his Muse, "Though nor in tune, nor wing, she reach thy Larke, / Her Lyrick feet may dance before the Arke" (ll. 13 - 14). Reviving the old pun on sun / Son, he fancies that the eyes of his Muse, "Now hunting Glow-wormes, may adore the Sun" (l. 16). Her "earthly" flame of inspiration may be devoured by a "pure flame . . . shot by Almighty power" (ll. 17 - 18), and thus his own eyes "in penitentiall dew may steepe / That brine, which they for sensuall love did weepe" (ll. 19 - 20). The use of *may* keeps the whole in the realm of conjecture, and Carew admits that it is " 'gainst Natures course" (l. 21) to quench fire with fire or water with water. Again, the *perhaps* indicates that he is making no declaration of change, only a declaration that he *could* change:

> Perhaps my restlesse soule, tyr'de with persuit
> Of mortall beauty, seeking without fruit
> Contentment there, which hath not, when enjoy'd,
> Quencht all her thirst, nor satisfi'd, though cloy'd;
> Weary of her vaine search below, Above
> In the first Faire may find th' immortall Love.
> Prompted by thy example then, no more
> In moulds of clay will I my God adore;
> But teare those Idols from my heart, and write
> What his blest Spirit, not fond Love shall indite;
> Then, I no more shall court the verdant Bay,
> But the dry leavelesse Trunke on *Golgotha;*
> And rather strive to gaine from thence one Thorne,
> Then all the flourishing wreathes by Laureats worne.
>   (ll. 23 - 36)

As Professor Joseph Summers points out, the "language clearly implies the unreality of the proposal. . . . There is surely little danger that anyone will become a religious poet who conceives of the decision only as the choice between a 'dry leaveless Trunk' and greenness."[7] Carew may have considered his own translation of the Psalms and his salute (in pentameter couplets) to his friend's efforts to be sufficient examples of writing what God's "blest Spirit, not fond Love shall indite."

Carew's poetry is also categorized in "Obsequies to the Lady Anne Hay" (67 - 68). His problem is to write about a distant cousin he has never seen, but one who evokes an expected series of images, especially the *gem* from the *casket:*

> I that ne're more of private sorrow knew
> Then from my Pen some froward Mistresse drew,
> And for the publike woe, had my dull sense
> So sear'd with ever adverse influence,
> As the invaders sword might have, unfelt,
> Pierc'd my dead bosome, yet began to melt:

Griefe's strong instinct, did to my blood suggest
In the unknowne losse peculiar interest.
But when I heard, the noble *Carlil's* Gemme,
The fayrest branch of *Dennye's* ancient stemme
Was from that Casket stolne, from this Trunke torne,
I found just cause, why they, why I should mourne.
(ll. 7 - 18)

What alternatives are available to a poet in such a situation? He
can, like "Apelles" (l. 25; really Zeuxis), draw on all of Nature to
figure "one Venus" (l. 28) and call her Anne Hay. Or he can write a
poem strung together with observations on all "the Worthies of her
sex" (l. 30) and claim that this is she. Or he can fashion the strict
religious life and say this was hers had she lived (ll. 33 - 38).
Abruptly and shatteringly, he dismisses these approaches as un-
worthy:

These are dull wayes, by which base pens, for hire,
Dawbe glorious vice, and from *Apollo's* quire
Steale holy Dittyes, which prophanely they
Upon the herse of every strumpet lay. . . .
(ll. 39 - 42)

He is back to his old distinction between good and bad poetry:

We will not bathe thy corps with a forc'd teare,
Nor shall thy traine borrow the blacks they weare:
Such vulgar spice, and gums, embalme not thee,
Thou art the Theame of Truth, not [of bad] Poetrie.[8]
(ll. 43 - 46)

He opts for letting her beauties and virtues be told in the features
and lives of her peers, whose inclination to jealousy of her, thus
overcome, will only prove her great worth (ll. 47 - 66). Again, false
poets are rebuked:

This shall gaine credit with succeeding times,
When nor by bribed pens, nor partiall rimes
Of engag'd kindred, but the sacred truth
Is storied by the partners of thy youth;
Their breath shall Saint thee, and be this thy pride,
Thus even by Rivals to be Deifide.
(ll. 69 - 74)

The situation is very similar to that of the "refusal-to-write-an-elegy" on Gustavus Adolphus; under the pretense of refusing, he writes, in his usual pentameter couplets, a new kind of elegy. He disavows any part in standard funereal poems (as he shows how familiar he is with those being written by his contemporaries and by himself on occasion) but writes one as he pretends to "plan" a novel way to commemorate Anne Hay. The assumed ploy of relegating the subject to chronicles and journals in "In answer of an Elegiacall Letter upon the death of the King of Sweden . . ." yields to a kindred notion in "Obsequies to the Lady Anne Hay"—the lady's fame will be emblazoned in her living "sisters," who will "raise / A glorious journall of thy thrifty dayes" (ll. 63 - 64). Only *self-serving* poetry is criticized in these pretended recourses to "chronicles" and "journals." The route he ascends from the possibilities of writing "their" (false) poetry to his kind is marked by the personal pronouns. He refers to himself as "I" while enumerating the alternatives, then shifts to "we" (l. 43) when his course is determined, a shift whose effect is similar to that of the royal *we*.

When his friend Aurelian Townshend invites him to write the elegy on Gustavus Adolphus (74 - 76), who was killed at Lützen on November 6, 1632, Carew, in his answer, asserts the public responsibility of the poet and describes his own limited range:

> . . . Alas! how may
> My Lyrique feet, that of the smooth soft way
> Of Love, and Beautie, onely know the tread,
> In dancing paces celebrate the dead
> Victorious King, or his Majesticke Hearse
> Prophane with th' humble touch of their low verse?
> (ll. 5 - 10)

After making his case for delivering the Swedish King to chronicles and journals (ll. 11 - 44), Carew insists that English poets must write of English conditions. He and Townshend and their fellow poets must mirror the peace that King Charles has given them or court disasters comparable to those that plagued Gustavus Adolphus. By praising peace and recording the pastimes allowable during these halcyon days, he seems to imply, the poet helps to insure their continuance:

> But let us that in myrtle bowers sit
> Under secure shades, use the benefit
> Of peace and plenty, which the blessed hand
> Of our good King gives this obdurate Land,
> Let us of Revels sing, and let thy breath
> (Which fill'd Fames trumpet with *Gustavus* death,
> Blowing his name to heaven) gently inspire
> Thy past'rall pipe, till all our swaines admire
> Thy song and subject, whilst they both comprise
> The beauties of the SHEPHERDS PARADISE. . . .[9]
>   (ll. 45 - 54)

This sense of public responsibility is not often sounded in Carew's poetry and calls to mind the tone of Jonson's country-house poems.

In praising Townshend's poetic powers, Carew is really indicating his own, though he pretends that his performance cannot match that of Townshend (ll. 55 - 59). One wonders just how "smooth" Townshend's verses were considered to be! Also, in the rather lengthy description of Townshend's masque, *Tempe Restord* (ll. 59 - 88), Carew indicates what he appreciates in poetry:

> For who like thee (whose loose discourse is farre
> More neate and polisht then our Poems are,
> Whose very gate's more gracefull then our dance)
> In sweetly-flowing numbers may advance
> The glorious night? When, not to act foule rapes,
> Like birds, or beasts, but in their Angel-shapes
> A troope of Deities came downe to guide
> Our steerelesse barkes in passions swelling tide
> By vertues Carde, and brought us from above
> A patterne of their owne celestiall love.
> Nor lay it in darke sullen precepts drown'd
> But with rich fancie, and cleare Action crown'd
> Through a misterious fable (that was drawne
> Like a transparant veyle of purest Lawne
> Before their dazelling beauties) the divine
> *Venus*, did with her heavenly *Cupid* shine.
> The stories curious web, the Masculine stile,
> The subtile sence, did Time and sleepe beguile,
> Pinnion'd and charm'd they stood to gaze upon
> Th' Angellike formes, gestures, and motion,
> To heare those ravishing sounds that did dispence
> Knowledge and pleasure, to the soule, and sense.
>   (ll. 55 - 76)

What he has praised is the Classical line of Jonson—graceful verses, clarity, beauty, a dual commitment to instilling knowledge and pleasure. Particularly noteworthy here is the praise of the "Masculine stile" (l. 75), for Jonson thought of himself as writing it too, though it is usually more closely associated with the "strong lines" of Donne. Carew in fact might almost be rebuking Donne with "darke sullen precepts drown'd." However, the scrutiny, the intellectual approach, and the overflowing of the pentameter couplets into long periodic sentences are more Donnean than Jonsonian.

The patriotic note of ll. 87 - 92, a reference to the performance of Henrietta Maria in Townshend's masque, leads into the last stanza, where, as one critic puts it, Carew "sum[s] up with great felicity the mood of make-believe and play-acting which was to be the undoing of King Charles . . .":[10]

> . . . these are subjects proper to our clyme.
> Tourneyes, Masques, Theaters, better become
> Our *Halcyon* dayes; what though the German Drum
> Bellow for freedome and revenge, the noyse
> Concernes not us, nor should divert our joyes;
> Nor ought the thunder of their Carabins
> Drowne the sweet Ayres of our tun'd Violins;
> Beleeve me friend, if their prevailing powers
> Gaine them a calme securitie like ours,
> They'le hang their Armes up on the Olive bough,
> And dance, and revell then, as we doe now.
> (ll. 94 - 104)

It may be foolhardy, particularly in a time like Carew's, on the verge of civil war, to see poetry's task as reflecting rather than correcting its milieu, but Carew apparently is sincere; his Royalism has overridden his common sense. While "philosophy" is not often the subject matter of his poems—and very few, considering how partisan the Cavaliers were, even touch on "politics"—he cannot be faulted for inconsistency. Time and again, the poems mirror his age and the frivolity of Charles's court, though, as has been shown, his eye is frequently also upon the ideals of poetry.

More typical is his use of poetry to vent his own "grief" or to persuade his mistress to love, as he indicates in a poem that does elegiac service to the notorious Lady Peniston, "An Elegie on the La: Pen: sent to my Mistresse out of France" (19 - 21):

Let him, who banisht farre from her deere sight
Whom his soule loves, doth in that absence write
Or lines of passion, or some powerfull charmes,
To vent his owne griefe, or unlock her armes;
Take off his pen, and in sad verse bemone
This generall sorrow, and forget his owne;
So may those Verses live, which else must dye;
For though the Muses give eternitie
When they embalme with verse, yet she could give
Life unto that Muse, by which others live.

But I must weepe no more over this urne,
My teares to their owne chanell must returne;
And having ended these sad obsequies,
My Muse must back to her old exercise,
To tell the story of my martyrdome. . . .
                    (ll. 7 - 16, 67 - 71)

Accustomed to writing "lines of passion, or some powerfull
charmes, / To vent his owne griefe, or unlock her armes," he now
takes time off to write an elegy, which not only has a public purpose
(to bemoan "This generall sorrow"), but will also help him forget
his being banished by his mistress.

Carew alludes too to different kinds of poetry. Good verse, he implies, endures because, partially at least, it treats worthy subjects.
(It is unfortunate that Carew chose to get into this topic when his
own subject was suspect!) The Muses immortalize through poetry
("embalme with verse"), true, but bad poetry does not survive.
Lady Peniston can give life to the verses of lesser poets because her
greatness will heighten their efforts. Nonetheless, when his own
obsequies are ended, his "Muse must back to her old exercise, / To
tell the story of my martyrdome [in love]." Careful poets will know,
however, that this tomb is sacred to the Muses and will know why
the "minions of the Muses" worship there.

If Carew had not been serious about poetry elsewhere, one would
have to overlook the comments in "An Elegie on the La:
Pen: . . ." as a superficial discharge of the duties of the court poet.
As is rather frequently the case in Carew's verses, however, the
reader senses a tension between the subject matter and the poet's
attitude toward it. The poet is again in rebellion against the conventions of the poetry he was expected to write.

II *Donne, Jonson, and Others*

A. *On John Donne*

Carew's most important poem is "An Elegie upon the death of the Deane of Pauls, Dr. John Donne" (71 - 74), printed in 1633, though probably written soon after Donne's death on March 31, 1631. The critical assessment of Donne in this verse-epistle still holds, and it is written for the most part in Donne's own style. Also, the observations made by Carew are now considered characteristics of the Donnean "strong-lined,"[11] Metaphysical school: viz., (1) Donne has purged poetry of the Renaissance reliance on imitation, especially of Greek and Latin authors; (2) he has inaugurated the reign of "masculine expression" or strong lines; (3) he has written poetry that has more than surface prettiness; (4) he has established "strict lawes" for poets, who must have not only pleasing words but "sense"—must appeal not only to the outer but to the inner senses; (5) he has banned the figures of Classical and Ovidian myth as the whole subject matter of poetry; and (6) he has become the "monarch of wit," and wit is at ease with poetry.

Carew maintains that, with the death of John Donne, poetry is "widdowed" and that those would-be poets left behind dare not offer elegies even in "unkneaded dowe-bak't prose" (l. 4). The pulpit, where Donne also excelled, may continue to function, but the "flame" of Donne's inspiration has been transformed, along with that of his Promethean breath, which inspired the "Delphique quire" (l. 22), into funeral flames. Like the pulpit, verse will maintain itself, but just barely, for even Donne must yield to Time and (in one of the most perceptive comments of its kind in the seventeenth century) to the "blinde fate of language":

> Thou shalt yield no precedence, but of time,
> And the blinde fate of language, whose tun'd chime
> More charmes the outward sense; Yet thou maist claime
> From so great disadvantage greater fame,
> Since to the awe of thy imperious wit
> Our stubborne language bends, made only fit
> With her tough-thick-rib'd hoopes to gird about
> Thy Giant phansie, which had prov'd too stout
> For their soft melting Phrases. As in time
> They had the start, so did they cull the prime
> Buds of invention many a hundred yeare,

And left the rifled fields, besides the feare
To touch their Harvest, yet from those bare lands
Of what is purely thine, thy only hands
(And that thy smallest worke) have gleaned more
Then all those times, and tongues could reape before. . . .
(ll. 45 - 60)

The reformation of verse represented in Donne's poetry will come
to a halt now; "The death of all the Arts" (l. 76) is here. Already his
admirer's elegy breaks the silence "with untun'd verse" (l. 71), a
testimony to the fast fading of Donne's influence. As if tired with
the useless effort now that his pattern (Donne) is receding, Carew
gives up trying to capture all of Donne's perfections or trying to
"weepe all our losse" (l. 88).[12] Yet in one incisive epitaph, he cap-
tures Donne's spirit better perhaps than anyone since:

Here lies a King, that rul'd as hee thought fit
The universall Monarchy of wit;
Here lie two Flamens, and both those, the best,
Apollo's first, at last, the true Gods Priest.
(ll. 95 - 98)

As has been pointed out,[13] in praising Donne, Carew must dis-
praise himself. He does use, even in this poem, Classical allusions;
he does write "soft melting Phrases" (l. 53); and he is surely an im-
itator. As to the last charge, he has written not only in the style of
Donne here, especially ll. 1 - 10, with their couplets flowing over
into sentences and their harsh consonants and heavy stresses, but in
the style of Jonson: ll. 95 - 98, for example, have the clarity and flow
of Jonson (and of Carew's own most constant style).

In fact, his greatest capabilities, in addition to his critical perception, fall within his imitation of Donne. He cultivates in this poem
the Metaphysical style and closely approximates Donne at his most
Metaphysical (verse that is closely wrought, argumentative, conversational, and intellectual, with strident rhythms to reinforce the
points and with images and themes rarely appearing in the poetry
of the day).[14] He puns in the best Donnean manner (e. g., *unkneaded*, l. 4; *dispense*, l. 9; *tyre*, l. 92), and he adopts images and
subjects from Donne's poetry. For example, playing on Donne's
own "Nor ever chaste, except you ravish mee" ("Holy Sonnet
XIV"), Carew acknowledges that Donne through his preaching
"Committed holy Rapes upon our Will" (l. 17). Donne's presenta-

tion of the "glimmering light," of "a kinde of World remaining still," after the loss of Elizabeth Drury ("The First Anniversary," ll. 70, 67), is brought to mind in Carew's description of the waning influence of the now dead Donne:

> Oh, pardon mee, that breake with untun'd verse
> The reverend silence that attends thy herse,
> Whose awfull solemne murmures were to thee
> More then these faint lines, A loud Elegie,
> That did proclaime in a dumbe eloquence
> The death of all the Arts, whose influence
> Growne feeble, in these panting numbers lies
> Gasping short winded Accents, and so dies:
> So doth the swiftly turning wheele not stand
> In th' instant we withdraw the moving hand,
> But some small time maintaine a faint weake course
> By vertue of the first impulsive force:
> And so whil'st I cast on thy funerall pile
> Thy crowne of Bayes, Oh, let it crack a while,
> And spit disdaine, till the devouring flashes
> Suck all the moysture up, then turne to ashes.
>   (ll. 71 - 86)

In addition to the theme of this section displaying Carew's knowledge of Donne's works, its technique reveals that Carew has absorbed as well as read his mentor. The conceit of the inertia of the wheel applied to the gradual waning of Donne's influence is of exactly the Metaphysical nature that Donne himself might have chosen; it is an apt and simultaneously unlikely analogy, appealing to the fancy and the intellect at once.

That same passage may be the best example of Donnean wit in the whole poem. Donne liked to refer to the phoenix, from whose ashes a new bird would rise. In l. 86 of Carew's poem, the ashes are present. Could it be that the implicit phoenix is Thomas Carew, who proves with this poem that he is much more than on the fringe of the Donne tradition? He surely knew and used Donne's imagery; in this elegy, for example, he alludes to the alchemical images (ll. 42, 68) that were favorites with Donne and that Carew himself used with some frequency. Moreover, it is unusual for the elegy to address the dead person rather than to eulogize him. Carew disavows eulogy and claims to have written only a short epitaph:

> I will not draw the envy to engrosse
> All thy perfections, or weepe all our losse;
> Those are too numerous for an Elegie,
> And this too great, to be express'd by mee.
> Though every pen should share a distinct part,
> Yet art thou Theme enough to tyre all Art;
> Let others carve the rest, it shall suffice
> I on thy Tombe this Epitaph incise.
>   (ll. 87 - 94)

As in the case of the elegy of Gustavus Adolphus, however, he has surely written elegy under the guise of not writing it. Here he has proved that good poetry can be produced though John Donne is dead, and that is not all; he has shown that Donne's own kind of poetry can be produced. Lest his wit in becoming the phoenix that springs from Donne's ashes be indecorous, he establishes the elegy as an invocation to the spirit of Donne. If he has become a Donnean poet then, he can modestly claim that Donne is responsible, not Thomas Carew.

Surely such a claim for Carew's wit is not outrageous beside, as one example, the "epitaph" he has produced for Donne—the words at the ends of its four lines summarize Carew's claims for Donne, "fit wit" and "best Priest." To insure that the "wit" here is noticed, he has, for the first time in the poem, faulted in the couplet rhyme ("best-Priest").

Carew has often tried for the intellectual voice of Donne in his poetry but has usually gained it only at the expense of thrusting the subject (most often the mistress) out of the central focus (e.g., "My mistris commanding me to returne her letters"). Here, however, in the pentameter couplets that spill over into long sentences, virtually into verse paragraphs, Carew has mastered the tough, probing style of Donne's satires. One instinctively feels that Carew has finally found the balance he has long sought. It is no little achievement to have summed Renaissance poetry and assessed the different style of John Donne; it is no little achievement to have understood his own ways in poetry and his own ambitions in it. He seems in the elegy on Donne to have made his peace with the supple verse that is his métier and with the Donnean line he admires most. He can be both Jonsonian and Donnean; he can write gracefully about matters intellectual. Yet, as Carew says in "In answer of an Elegiacall Letter upon the death of the King of Sweden . . . ," he continued to feel that Donne was "worth all that went before" (l. 12). The wistful note in the elegy on Donne is one of its many assets. One can only wish that it were possible to date Carew's poems in order to determine whether his achievement of his own sense of balance in the Donne elegy affected the poems that followed it.

B. *On Ben Jonson*

"Great *Johnsons* verse," as Carew refers to it in l. 32 of "To my worthy Friend, M. D'avenant, Upon his Excellent Play, the *Just Italian*" (95 - 96), is, as has been shown, a second major influence on the poetry of Thomas Carew, one of the "Tribe of Ben." James Howell's report of Carew's comment at Jonson's dinner party proves him no intimidated follower of Jonson. That view is reinforced by his "To Ben. Johnson. Upon occasion of his Ode of defiance annext to his Play of the new Inne" (64 - 65).

At the first performance of *The New Inn* in 1629, the play was "hissed" from the stage. Jonson brooded and sought revenge against the players and the audience. At its publication in 1631, it is presented "As it was never acted, but most negligently play'd, by some, the Kings Servants." The volume also contained a vituperative poem (described as "The just indignation the Author tooke at the vulgar censure of his Play, by some malicious spectators. . . .") attacking the taste of the "lothsome age." Carew's poem is a response to Jonson's poetic and the subsequent public outrage.

Carew informs "deare Ben" that while his chastisement of "the sotted Age" for its pride and "empty scribbling" has been proper, there *has* been a decline of Jonson's "commique Muse from the exalted line / Toucht by thy *Alchymist*" (ll. 5 - 6). Carew rushes nevertheless to reassure Jonson with a bit of the "unnatural natural history" of which Carew was fond, that "all thy Eaglets [works] may / Endure the Sunnie tryall" (ll. 11 - 12). Besides, "Who hath his flock of cackling Geese compar'd / With thy tun'd quire of Swans?" (ll. 15 - 16).[15] No author should expect (witness Carew's own!) a perfect evenness of performance among all of his works, as Carew calls on his legal background to explain:

> Nor thinke it much (since all thy Eaglets may
> Endure the Sunnie tryall) if we say
> This hath the stronger wing, or that doth shine
> Trickt up in fairer plumes, since all are thine;
> Who hath his flock of cackling Geese compar'd

> With thy tun'd quire of Swans? or else who dar'd
> To call thy births deformed? but if thou bind
> By Citie-custome, or by *Gavell-kind,*
> In equall shares thy love on all thy race,
> We may distinguish of their sexe, and place;
> Though one hand form them, & though one brain strike
> Soules into all, they are not all alike.
>   (ll. 11 - 22)

Moreover, Jonson's rage is unseemly, "immodest"; it "proclaimes thy ytch of praise" (l. 26). Let the detractors rage that Jonson is slow at composition, that he plagiarizes "martyr'd Authors." The true test of authority is endurance (ll. 23 - 46).

Having skillfully reminded Jonson that no one is without fault—how many times has he heard these same charges, after all? Why so outraged now?—Carew reminds him that the *worthy* audience thinks none greater: "The wiser world doth greater Thee confesse / Then all men else, then Thy selfe onely lesse" (ll. 49 - 50). Carew reiterates the criticism implied throughout the poem: Jonson's immoderate outbursts betray his insecurity. As a critic himself and one of the "wiser world," he should know the value of his performances and remain aloof from vulgar reproofs.

How Jonson received Carew's criticism in this poem is not known. At his mentor's death, however, Carew did not contribute to the memorial volume, *Jonsonus Virbius* (1638). Despite the fact that Viscount Falkland's own poetical contribution to that collection anticipates a poem from Carew, it was not forthcoming.

Carew is less concerned in "To Ben. Johnson . . ." to capture the subject's style. He does allude to the "Sons of Ben," but in a legal image (*gavelkind,* the division of an estate equally among the heirs, l. 18) more consonant with his own custom than with Jonson's. For the most part here, he is a follower of Donne: in the persuasive argument of the pentameter couplets; in the conversational, at times colloquial language (e.g., "Trickt up," l. 14; "cackling Geese," l. 15); in the pun of "houres" / whores (l. 46); and especially in the series of short but vividly drawn images as analogies (evening, ll. 6 - 10; birds, ll. 11 - 16; "Citie-custome" and "Gavell-kind," ll. 17 - 19; sands, ll. 30 - 32; lamp, ll. 32 - 37; and "bootie," ll. 40 - 42). Carew is his own man in the manipulation of the contrasting frames of reference: "the sotted Age" versus "we" versus "thou." Thus, decorously, he places himself somewhere between the "cackling Geese" who are bad critics, bad poets, and a bad audience and the swans and eagles who are Jonson himself. Not so decorous is his tendency to follow a brief statement of negation of the age with a longer, though carefully considered, chastisement of Jonson himself.

As with the Donne elegy, Carew does reveal that he knows Jonson's method and the contemporary commentaries on it. He praises the plain style for which Jonson was famous by contrasting it with "knottie" writing (ll. 39 - 40). More interesting is the fact that the charges Carew lists as having been leveled by Jonson's critics can as easily be applied to Carew himself. His Muse was known to be "hide-bound"; and, though it is not a public criticism directed against Carew personally, he is as much a "plagiarist" as Jonson. Carew also knew the importance of the "fit audience . . . though few" and tries to remind Jonson of this kind of forum throughout the poem.

Carew could not have been unaware that many of the comments about Jonson's poetry were equally applied to or could be equally applied to his own. This verse-epistle to Ben Jonson, along with the elegy to Donne, gave him the opportunity, rare in his age, for self-assessment and for critical comprehension of another great poetic school at work at the moment. If one remembers how long the time lag usually is between the formation of a literary school and critical recognition of that school, he or she will perceive the uniqueness of Carew's situation. Before and during Carew's time, most of what could be construed as criticism was either adulatory or vituperative. Seldom was there an attempt to comprehend whole literary movements, as the Jonsonian or Donnean lines. Seldom was there an attempt by a poet to seek an understanding of his own place in relation to the larger currents at work in his period.

C.   *Critical Comments on Others and Contributions to Plays*

Other Carew poems rather facilely commend the plays and works of his friends and of public figures or provide tidbits for those works. Negligible for the most part and adulatory in a conventional way, this group does show labor as well as his continuous involvement in court productions. Occasionally there are echoes of his better-known poems.

For some apparently lost play at Whitehall Palace, Carew provided "Foure Songs by way of *Chorus* to a play, at an entertainment of the King and Queene, by my Lord Chamberlaine . . ." (59 - 62), two other "Songs in the Play" (63 - 64), and probably the prologue

(127) and epilogue (127 - 28) as well. The first choral song,
"Jealousie" (59 - 60), is interesting primarily for biographical
reasons; it is the poem written at the request of Thomas Killigrew to
settle his quarrel with Cecilia Crofts. Worth considering are the
answers to the last two questions of this dialogue in tetrameter
couplets:

> Quest. Oh how can such a spurious line
> Proceed from Parents so divine?
>   Ans. As streames, which from their Crystall spring
> Doe sweet and cleare their waters bring,
> Yet mingling with the brackish maine,
> Nor taste, nor colour they retaine.
>   Qu. Yet Rivers 'twixt their own bankes flow
> Still fresh, can jealousie doe so?
>   An. Yes, whilst shee keepes the stedfast ground
> Of Hope, and Feare, her equall bound;
> Hope sprung from favour, worth, or chance,
> Towar'ds the faire object doth advance;
> Whil'st Feare, as watchfull Sentinell
> Doth the invading Foe repell;
> And Jealousie thus mixt, doth prove
> The season, and the salt of love:
> But when Feare takes a larger scope,
> Stifling the child of Reason, Hope,
> Then sitting on th' usurped throne,
> She like a Tyrant rules alone,
> As the wilde Ocean unconfin'de,
> And raging as the Northern-winde.
>   (ll. 21 - 42).

The first answer employs another of the water analogies that Carew
favored, as in the more famous "To my Mistris sitting by a Rivers
side. An Eddy" (14). Carew's careful scrutiny and versatility are displayed here, however, for the conceit of the courtship between river
and bank is altered to account for the descent of jealousy from Love
as sweet and brackish waters mingle.

Carew also liked to examine an image or a conceit at length. Having taken the mingled waters as far as he can, he yet manages to extend his argument by turning once more, in the second answer, to a
consideration of "means and extremes," treated, for example, in
"Mediocritie in love rejected" (12 - 13). So long as Jealousy is
caught equally between Hope and Fear, it can "prove / The season,

and the salt of love." Slipping toward either extreme, it becomes the monster the world knows. The pun on "season" and the carefully argued approach, both influenced by Donne, are also typical Carew features. Were this merely a light and witty response to a friend's request, the close argument would probably not be present. As the poem stands, the reader feels that Carew has worked to produce this "command performance" as Pope was to work to produce "The Rape of the Lock" under similar circumstances. Carew cannot be dismissed as a frivolous poet on an occasion when the poetry demanded could have been potentially his most frivolous.

The second choral song (for the nonextant play), "Feminine Honour" (60 - 61), offers comparison with one of Carew's most widely known poems as it presents an additional portrait of the "Gyant, Honour," whose "huge Collosses legs" are violated every day by the bold lovers described in "A Rapture" (49 - 53):

> Oh haplesse sex! Unequall sway
> > Of partiall Honour! Who may know
> Rebels from subjects that obey,
> > When malice can on vestals throw
> Disgrace, and Fame fixe high repute
> On the close shamelesse Prostitute?
>
> Vaine Honour! thou art but disguise,
> > A cheating voyce, a jugling art,
> No judge of vertue, whose pure eyes
> > Court her own Image in the heart,
> More pleas'd with her true figure there,
> Then her false Eccho in the eare.
> > (ll. 13 - 24)

Again, one is struck with the care Carew has taken in these minor contributions to a play not his own. The personification of Honor is extended through two verses, and Carew has varied the presentation by describing its effect on the "haplesse sex" in Stanza 3 and then rebuking it directly in Stanza 4. The abstraction comes to full life in the latter.

Similarly, in the first stanza, an abstraction is brought to life by concrete images as Carew reconsiders attitudes toward love in former ages (a reminiscence of "Loves Force," 116):

> In what esteeme did the Gods hold
> > Faire Innocence, and the chaste bed,
> When scandall'd vertue might be bold
> > Bare-foot, upon sharpe Cultures [ploughshares], spread
> O're burning coles to march, yet feele
> Nor scorching fire, nor piercing steele?

Within the stanza itself, there are sharp contrasts, as the juxtaposition of the abstract Innocence and the concrete "chaste bed"; the personification of the abstraction Virtue going "bare-foot"; the oxymoron of "scandall'd vertue"; and the simple contrast of fire and steel. In the second stanza, contrast becomes more prominent in the striking image of "Why, when the hard edg'd Iron did turne / Soft as a bed of Roses blowne" (ll. 7 - 8), a pivot for the greatest contrast and the central question of the poem: why

> > > . . . should man alone
> > 'Gainst female Innocence conspire,
> > Harder then steele, fiercer then fire?
> > > (ll. 10 - 12)

"Separation of Lovers" (61 - 62), the third choral song, resalutes a favorite Carew borrowing: that true love may enter through the sight, but it also engages the mind (ll. 5 - 8). He insists, as Donne would, that "mind-love" cannot thrive without "body-love":

> > For the sense not fed, denies
> > > Nourishment unto the minde,
> > > Which with expectation pinde,
> > Love of a consumption dyes.
> > > (ll. 21 - 24)

In addition to this abstract idea, the poem makes use of the cliché that "absence makes the heart grow fonder": "Yet though absence for a space, / Sharpen the keene Appetite . . ." (ll. 17 - 18). It goes on to qualify that conclusion, however, with "Long continuance, doth quite / All Loves characters efface" (ll. 19 - 20). Present, too, are sharply delineated images that offer relief from abstraction and conventional materials. Love is at once personified and activated by being endowed with "an hungrie eye" that "Glut[s] on Beautie" (ll. 13 - 14). The animal images of the first stanza inform the title and subject of the poem as nothing else could do:

> Stop the chafed Bore, or play
> With the Lyons paw, yet feare
> From the Lovers side to teare
> Th'Idoll of his soule away.

In fact, there is a witty and well-planned alternation of abstract and concrete verses; and their complexity is further heightened by links from one abstract stanza to another and from one concrete stanza to another. Stanzas 1 and 4 are linked by their concrete images and the slight variation in their subject matter; Stanzas 2 and 6 are linked by their abstract ideas; Stanzas 3 and 5 are linked even more closely as ll. 17 and 18 actually negotiate between them. It is as if Carew by these linking stanzas meant to emphasize and demonstrate the ill nature of the subject defined in the title: "Separation of Lovers." The other peculiar feature of this little poem results from the same combination of abstract and concrete. Stanzas 1 and 4 in their defining images stand in the sharpest contrast to the philosophical, argumentative cast of the remaining four stanzas. Carew seems intent on displaying the two major techniques he exploits in his poetry.

A similar view of love as the product of mind and body is presented in the fourth choral song, "Incommunicabilitie of Love" (62):

> Qu. Whence springs love? An. From beauty.
>   Qu. Why
> Should th' effect not multiply
> As fast i' th' heart, as doth the cause i' th' eye?
>
> An. When two Beauties equall are,
>   Sense preferring neither fayre,
> Desire stands still, distracted 'twixt the paire.
>   (ll. 10 - 15)

The image of love suspended between two beauties recalls again the means-extremes question of "Jealousie." This poem, under the influence of Donne, offers an interesting comparison as well with the situation Carew is trying to work out in "To T. H. a Lady resembling my Mistresse" (26 - 27). Again, it effects a strange combination of abstract and concrete, the former this time predominant. The abstract, discursive approach is broken only twice. In the first instance, Love is visualized as having a "twinn'd-flame" and a

"forked dart" (l. 8). In the second, the paralysis of Love "distracted
'twixt" two "Beauties equall" is likened to a wolf unable to choose
between "Two fayre Lambes":

> So in equall distance lay
> Two fayre Lambes in the Wolfe's way;
> The hungry beast will sterve e're chuse his prey.
>   (ll. 16 - 18)[16]

Not only does the analogy explain the abstraction of Love; it sounds
a somewhat typically cynical note in Carew as the predatory image
reminds the questioner once again (as in ll. 7 - 9) that "wilde lust"
and not love *can* possess the heart.

The two songs, "A Lover in the disguise of an Amazon, is dearly
beloved of his Mistresse" (63) and "A Lady rescued from death by a
Knight, who in the instant leaves her, complaines thus" (63 - 64),
show a continuing attempt by Carew to put himself in the woman's
place.[17] The first, with the lover disguised as an Amazon, offers a
rather wild twist on the motif of equal love versus disdain:

> Cease in cold jealous feares to pine
> Sad wretch, whom Rivals undermine;
> For though I hold lockt in mine armes
> My lifes sole joy, a Traytors charmes
> Prevaile, whilst I may onely blame
> My selfe, that myne owne Rivall am.
>   (ll. 13 - 18)

The lover is beloved but only because he is disguised as an Amazon
in this poem that recalls some of the complications of disguise in
Shakespeare's plays. Clever here is the fact that the speaker finds
himself beset by the same old Petrarchan oxymora:

> Cease, Beauties exile to lament
> The frozen shades of banishment,
> For I in that faire bosome dwell
> That is my Paradise, and Hell;
> Banisht at home, at once at ease
> In the safe Port, and tost on Seas.
>   (ll. 7 - 12)

The second song for the play is threaded with the same
Petrarchan themes (the "light" but not the "heat" of her "Sun"

flees away, ll. 1 - 2; he rides away in a whirlwind yet remains "fixt" in her heart; "Love lent thee wings to flye, so Hee / Unfeather'd, now must rest with mee," ll. 11 - 12). It is the lady who complains, and with an intensity of passion not seen elsewhere in Carew's poems. In the midst of the well-worn images, she also manages to sound a beautifully appealing note:

> If thou repose in the moyst bed
>   Of the Sea-Queene, bring back the day
> To our darke clime, and thou shalt lye
> Bath'd in the sea flowes from mine eye.
>   (ll. 3 - 6)

Similarly, the final stanza brings a change to the conventional Cupid allusion:

> Helpe, helpe, brave Youth, I burne, I bleed,
>   The cruell God with Bow and Brand
> Pursues the life thy valour freed,
>   Disarme him with thy conquering hand;
> And that thou mayest the wilde boy tame
> Give me his dart, keepe Thou his flame.

In the midst of her passion, she will trick the knight into performing another "rescue" for her: if he does overcome Cupid and take his dart, she will shoot it into the disdainful lover, who will then burn as well as she. Her reference to the "Darke riddles of the amorous art" (l. 10) is fitting for her own case but might well serve as an umbrella too for many poems of the Carew canon.

The prologue to the play is an insignificant address to the King and Queen (127); it does employ an extended conceit (ll. 1 - 14) and a clever image ("To oyle the lazie Minutes as they slide," l. 18). The epilogue (127 - 28) deserves attention as a restatement of Carew's position on extremes and "in-between's":

> Hunger is sharp, the Sated Stomack dull,
> Feeding delights, t'wixt Emptiness and full:
> The pleasure lyes, not in the end, but streames
> That flowe betwixt two opposite Extreames.
> Soe doth the flux from hott to cold Combine
> An equall temper, such is noble wine
> Twixt fullsome Must and Vinegar too tart:
> Pleasures the scratching betwixt Itch and smart,

It is a shifting Tartar [a thief], that still flyes
From place to place, if it stand still it dyes;
After much rest labour delights, when paine
Succeeds long travaile rest growes sweete againe;
Paine is the base, on which his nimble feete
Move in contynuall chaunge from sower to sweete.
(ll. 1 - 14)

These analogues from Nature compose the preamble to the real
statement of the epilogue: the playwright "was Content this last
peece should grow sower / Onely to sweeten the Insueing hower"
(ll. 31 - 32). The unusual feature in this carefully argued, carefully
thought-out piece is the series of analogies Carew uses to build to
his point. Most often, he concentrates on exploring at length a
single image.

Besides their care and work, these contributions to others'
productions also demonstrate almost the full range of Carew's
metrical variations. The prologue and the epilogue are in pentameter couplets; "Jealousie" is in tetrameter couplets. "Feminine
Honour," "A Lover in the disguise of an Amazon . . . ," and "A
Lady rescued from death by a Knight . . ." use six-line tetrameter
stanzas; the first and the last employ ababcc rhyme schemes, but "A
Lover in the disguise of an Amazon . . ." is in couplets. "Separation of Lovers" is in quatrains or envelope stanzas (abba). Its
tetrameter lines make use of truncation to reinforce the theme. "Incommunicabilitie of Love" returns to tercets (aaa) but combines
pentameter and tetrameter lines and uses truncation. These poems
are among Carew's most slender productions; yet in versification
and technique he has spared no attention.

Plays by Thomas May and William Davenant evoke some
worthwhile critical comments from Carew, both poems being in
pentameter couplets. May, one of the circle of friends Clarendon
describes as including Carew, introduced *The Heir* first on the
private stage. Carew's "To my Honoured friend, Master Thomas
May, upon his Comedie, *The Heire*" (92 - 93), the first of his works
to be published, was attached to the published version of the play in
1622. Wittily playing on the drama's title, Carew uses the metaphor
of the growing child as he writes to introduce this "heir" to the
public stage. The hierarchy of his considerations is worth noticing as
he moves from verse to language to plot in his commendations.
Moreover, his observations about May's verse could as easily summarize the major portion of his own:

> You shall observe his words in order meet,
> And softly stealing on with equall feet
> Slide into even numbers, with such grace
> As each word had beene moulded for that place.
>   (ll. 13 - 16)

Like Jonson's *The New Inn,* Davenant's *The Just Italian*[18] (published in 1630) was a stage failure; and Carew's title, "To my worthy Friend, M. D'avenant, Upon his Excellent Play, *The Just Italian"* (95 - 96), shows the poet's intention. Since he alludes to Jonson in it, he may have wanted to remind Davenant that public response was not always to be trusted. The condemnation of the "sullen Age" (l. 4) seems much more vehement than in the Jonson poem he was later to write. He delineates once more the wise and stupid audience. For the latter,

>   . . . marke the places
> Provoke their smiles, frownes, or distorted faces,
> When, they admire, nod, shake the head: they'le be
> A scene of myrth, a double Comedie.
>   (ll. 17 - 20)

The ordinary audience admires nothing "that exceeds Red Bull, and Cockpit flight" (l. 24), nothing of "serious sence" (l. 28), not even "The terser *Beaumonts* or great *Johnsons* verse" (l. 32). Davenant, like Jonson, must be content with the plaudits of "Wisemen" (l. 38). This "sullen Age" requires satire (ll. 4 - 5). It has not learned to judge literature properly and has banished "cleare, candid Ingenuitie" (l. 8); "Now noyse prevailes, and he is tax'd for drowth / Of wit, that with the crie, spends not his mouth" (ll. 13 - 14). Davenant's "cleere, yet loftie straine" only "Wisemen, that governe Fate, shall entertaine" (ll. 37 - 38).

Davenant, unless he took Carew's message to heart, must have been a disappointed writer. His play *The Witts,* licensed in 1633 / 34 and printed in 1636, received at best a mixed response. Carew's "To the Reader of Master William Davenant's Play" (97), the only commendatory poem published with it, draws an Horatian and a Jonsonian analogy between theatrical and culinary arts to promote Carew's view that wit (again with a glance at the play's ti-tle) demands circumspection. A spectator cannot condemn a play simply because it does not match his particular "taste." The lengthy, close pursuit of the analogy or "similie," as Carew calls it, is typical. Here it is in part:

> . . . So you may
> Affect a sad, merry, or humerous Play,
> If, though the kind distaste or please, the Good
> And Bad, be by your Judgment understood;
> But if, as in this Play, where with delight
> I feast my Epicurean appetite
> With rellishes so curious, as dispence
> The utmost pleasure to the ravisht sense,
> You should professe that you can nothing meet
> That hits your taste, either with sharpe or sweet,
> But cry out, 'tis insipid; your bold Tongue
> May doe it's Master, not the Author wrong;
> For Men of better Pallat will by it
> Take the just elevation of your Wit.
>   (ll. 17 - 30)

Carew claims that one's critical assessments redound on one's own head. Perhaps this perception accounts for the care he has lavished not only on the Donne and Jonson poems but on the contributions to others' works and on these public commendations.

In "To Will. Davenant my Friend" (98), also in the pentameter couplets Carew seems to have preferred for verse-epistles, he anticipates the criticism of Davenant's *Madagascar; with other Poems* (1638). The first thirteen lines justify Davenant's approach by implying that it is like that of Homer and Virgil. His defense of Davenant's mingling of romance and history stands in contrast to views in others of his poems:

> . . . What though Romances lye
> Thus blended with more faithfull Historie?
> Wee, of th' adult'rate mixture not complaine,
> But thence more Characters of Vertue gaine;
> More pregnant Patterns, of transcendent Worth,
> Than barren and insipid Truth brings forth:
> So, oft the Bastard nobler fortune meets,
> Than the dull Issue of the lawfull sheets.[19]
>   (ll. 13 - 20)

Only infrequently (e.g., the wolf image in "Incommunicabilitie of Love," ll. 16 - 18) does Carew reach farther than he should for the apt analogy. Here the analogy between the fine art of bastardizing and his friend's work is most humorous and indecorous.

Carew's comments on his friends and their works show his

allegiance to the colony of courtiers at the court of Charles I. Given his own masque, *Coelum Britannicum,* and his obvious interest in the theater, as evidenced in the poems of this section, one wonders why his talents were not turned more often to the stage. Again, there is a somewhat disappointing picture of the dilettante who wasted his powers for lack of focus. He has worked on these little poems and has voiced ideals in them, as elsewhere; but they lose force by the failure to pursue those critical perceptions more consistently. Except in the elegy on Donne, Carew himself did relatively little to educate the greater audience and bring it toward the "wiser world."

Another commendatory poem, "To my much honoured friend, Henry Lord Cary of Lepington, upon his translation of Malvezzi" (95), displays, for example, an attitude toward the problems inherent in language that recalls Carew's views in the Donne elegy and that shows his potential seriousness. What seems to be missing here and elsewhere from Carew's canon is any theorizing about the relation between language itself and his own kind of composition. The random commentaries in the poems show his capabilities, and the reader feels that he was sometimes uneasy about not making more of them. It is as if he were fearful of laying aside the mask of the amorous poet lest Jonson's pomposity overtake him.

CHAPTER 5

Carew's Occasional Poetry

I N a sense, all of Carew's work is "public" poetry, for the "darke riddles of the amorous art" (for example, the "private" poetry to Celia) used established poetic forms, were circulated in manuscript, and were accepted as part of the formal rites of courtship and gallantry practiced by the court circle of his day as part of the general trend toward *vers de société*. There is a group of poems, however, apart from the celebrations of Celia, of his "mistress," and of love at large, that is made up of *occasional* and public verse proper. These poems include the addresses to literary friends and figures and the salutes to their works discussed in Chapter 4. Considered here is the "social" poetry of commendation and friendship as Carew writes of friends and acquaintances in their homes, at special occasions (hence the term "occasional"), in courtships and marriages, in sickness, and in death.

I Gallantry to Fashionable Ladies

"A. L." and "A. D." remain unidentified, but represent, no doubt, typical objects of Carew's court gallantry. "To A. L. Perswasions to love" (4 - 6) immediately calls to mind Carew's Celia poem, "Perswasions to enjoy" (16), also in the frequent Cavalier vein of *carpe diem*, and offers comparison with Marvell's "To His Coy Mistress."[1] George Saintsbury's praises for it are typical:

It is an unwearying delight to read and re-read the . . . "Persuasions to Love." . . . That the sentiment is common enough matters little; the commonest things in poetry are always the best. But the delicate interchange of the catalectic and acatalectic dimeter [actually tetrameter with shifts to pentameter and some truncation], the wonderful plays and changes of cadence, the opening, as it were, of fresh stops at the beginning of each new paragraph of the verse, so that the music acquires a new colour, the

104

felicity of the several phrases, the cunning heightening of the passion as the poet comes to "Oh! love me then, and now begin it," and the dying fall of the close, make up to me, at least, most charming pastime. It is not the same kind of pleasure, no doubt, as that given . . . by such pieces as the great soliloquies of Shakespere. Any one may say . . . that it is not such a "high" kind. But it is a kind, and in that kind perfect.[2]

The achievement is especially impressive when one realizes that the major portion of the poem, beginning with l. 29, is a translation of Marino's *Bellezza Caduca*.[3]

The opening, "original" with Carew, combines admonition and compliment. The tired flatteries of suitors contain few truths:

> Thinke not cause men flatt'ring say,
> Y' are fresh as Aprill, sweet as May,
> Bright as is the morning starre,
> That you are so. . . .
>
> (ll. 1 - 4)

A. L.'s case, however, is different; she *is* beautiful. The lover-poet therefore can turn his argument in a different direction. Being fair, she must not be proud and disdainful, for her beauty is the gift of Nature; and the frequent Renaissance debate as to whether Nature's prodigality is to be mirrored by man has the poet standing for the affirmative. ("A. L." has neither the argumentative powers of the Lady in Milton's *Comus* nor the time to indulge in debate, so quickly does the speaker's "logic" move on.) Pressing her beauty as the gift of Nature again, he now points up the sin: "There to be scarce, where shee hath bin / So prodigall of her best graces" (ll. 12 - 13). "Common beauties, and meane faces" (l. 14) will triumph while she is "coy."

Her common sense is next appealed to. She will derive more pleasure in being "persuaded to love" than he. Enter the *carpe diem* motif via Marino: "Beautie's sweet, but beautie's fraile" (l. 32). All those physical perfections for which her "servant"-lovers praise her will fail, even the eye, "which now is *Cupids* nest" (l. 41), the latter an image of which Carew is seemingly fond. Again she is urged to be tutored by Nature. These suitors will "Like swallowes when your summers done, . . . flye and seeks some warmer Sun" (ll. 47 - 48). On the other hand, she must "like the Ant / In plenty hoord for time of scant" (ll. 53 - 54). Her discernment is subtly underscored as he urges her to choose one (him) who will "Love for an

age, not for a day" (l. 58). The source he calls upon to support his
case is intended to remind her of Time's decays: "And old folkes say
there are no paynes / Like itch of love in aged vaines" (ll. 67 - 68,
with a pun on "veins" and "in vain"). The final pitch is made with
"an urgency . . . too remarkable to omit":[4]

> Oh love me then, and now begin it,
> Let us not loose this present minute:
> For time and age will worke that wrack
> Which time or age shall ne're call backe.
> The snake each yeare fresh skin resumes,
> And Eagles change their aged plumes;
> The faded Rose each spring, receives
> A fresh red tincture on her leaves:
> But if your beauties once decay,
> You never know a second *May* [another pun: "youth" and "the
> ability to"].
> Oh, then be wise, and whilst your season
> Affords you dayes for sport, doe reason;
> Spend not in vaine your lives short houre,
> But crop in time your beauties flower:
> Which will away, and doth together
> Both bud, and fade, both blow and wither.
>   (ll. 69 - 84)

Again she is lessoned from Nature—but daringly the poet urges this
time how different she is from snake, eagle, and rose and yet how
like the last: budding, fading, blowing, withering. The whole argument is "seize the day while you can," the *carpe diem;* to develop
it, Carew has gone to a catalogue or an enumeration of analogies
from Nature. This is the love poem in which Carew has perhaps
best merged the argumentative, conversational tone of Donne and
his own graceful rhyming couplets (predominantly tetrameter but
with catalexis altering some lines to pentameter).

In "To A. D. unreasonable distrustfull of her owne beauty" (84 -
86), in pentameter couplets, the fault is with Doris's mirror, which
the poet therefore urges her to break under the conceit of an ob-
fuscating text. All beauties belong to her face, and if she cannot see
them, then the glass has been "suborn'd" (l. 8, another of Carew's
frequent legal images) to leave them out. Any blemishes she finds,
on the other hand, are due to the magic of her face, which has
"enchanted" the crystal glass and deludes her eyes "With ayrie
repercussive sorceries" (l. 16).

Yet another possibility occurs to him: the image has fallen in love with her and pines and grows pale and wan (like a sonnet lover). Dipping into Platonic lore, he concludes that she must thus know her true beauty (the cause) by its effects not only on the mirror image but on his "love-sick heart" (l. 23): "In that true mirrour see how fayre thou art" (l. 24), an argument he has also raised in "A Looking-Glasse" (19) and in "On his Mistres lookeinge in a glasse" (132). Her image in his heart gives him an opportunity to praise her in one of his well-used images ("Pearles, and Roses," l. 29) and to reassert the link between love and poetry: "Whilst Delfique Priests, (enlightened by their Theame) / In amorous numbers court thy golden beame" (ll. 31 - 32).

The Donnelike use of legal imagery and the close argument of the first part of the poem give way to one of the most densely packed and difficult passages Carew wrote as he seeks again to convince her of her beauty by proving it the "cause" of these "effects" (the "festring sore" of his heart, l. 41). The argument is so closely drawn that only a lengthy step-by-step examination could do it justice. Ultimately, however, it gives a modern turn to an "old" poem as it insists that "You undervalew me, when you bestow / On me, what you nor care for, nor yet know" (ll. 71 - 72). In a poignant note that has been prepared for by the title, he argues that she cannot love him until she loves herself. One is left with the distinct impression that there is more here than fashionable gallantry; Carew's psychological perceptiveness belies the simple amorous poet of reputation:

> I'le trade with no such Indian foole as sells
> Gold, Pearles, and pretious stones, for Beads and Bells;
> Nor will I take a present from your hand,
> Which you or prize not, or not understand;
> It not endeares your bountie that I doe
> Esteeme your gift, unlesse you doe so too;
> You undervalew me, when you bestow
> On me, what you nor care for, nor yet know.
> No (Lovely *Doris*) change thy thoughts, and be
> In love first with thy selfe, and then with me.
> You are afflicted that you are not faire,
> And I as much tormented that you are,
> What I admire, you scorne; what I love, hate,
> Through different faiths, both share an equall Fate,
> Fast to the truth, which you renounce, I stick,
> I dye a Martyr, you an Heretique.
> (ll. 65 - 80)

This final section has achieved the smooth, rational thrust that is lacking in the middle portion. It also demonstrates a topical approach (the reference to the Indians in ll. 65 - 66) rare in Carew.

II *Commendation of the Nobility and Greetings to Friends*

The good relations between Carew and Henrietta Maria, cemented first by his alleged saving of her reputation in the St. Albans episode, are suggested by the easy tetrameter couplets of "To the Queene" (90 - 91). Carew has in mind here her coterie of Platonic love,[5] for she rules not only England but the domain of Love, whose "prophaner Altars" (l. 5), in alternate lines, are contrasted with her "chaste beames" (l. 4). In a rebuke of Carew's own position in "A Rapture," "His [Love's] Kingdome knowes no rule but this, / *What ever pleaseth lawfull is*" (ll. 11 - 12). Under the Queen's sway, "the rude Male" (l. 15) is "satisfied / With one faire Female by his side"; and the sexes unite to "forme loves pure Hermophradite" (l. 18).[6] Her powers extend so far as to reform such creatures as the satyr and the centaur; and, in a bold image even for Carew, the other three elements are "inspired" by her "pregnant fire" (l. 29), more Neo-platonism and a continuation of the alchemical symbolism begun in "loves pure Hermophradite."

More carefully wrought is "To Master W. Mountague" (78 - 79), whose pentameter couplets use the legal jargon garnered from Carew's tenure at the Inns of Court and from Donne and other Renaissance poets. Artfully complimentary, Carew "arrests" Walter Montagu,[7] diplomat and friend of Queen Henrietta Maria, at the "countreyes suit" (l. 1). He complains of the state's loss with Montagu's departure and reverses the exile figure:

> This Kingdome lives in exile, and all hearts
> That rellish worth, or honour, being rent
> From your perfections, suffer banishment.
> These are your publike injuries. . . .
>
> (ll. 14 - 17)

In l. 17, Carew turns away to plead his private quarrel, swearing "By *Celia's* eyes" (l. 22) not to desist until he gains Montagu's heart as his friend has gained his. The mock-duel of the private quarrel permits him to finish in quip and pun: "So if you foyle me when we meet, I'le then / Give you fayre leave to wound me so agen" (ll. 29 - 30).

III *Country-House Poems*

Ben Jonson's influence on Carew becomes more specific in the "country-house" poems. Admiring the decorum and order of the Classical period, Jonson imitated, for example, Horace's celebration of his retreat to the Sabine Hills and Martial's description of the villa of Faustinus in his own ode "To Penshurst." The genre of documentary[8] or country-house or estate poetry presented the home under inspection as an emblem or symbol of political and personal rectitude, made so by the aristocratic family who occupied the estate.

Horace, Martial, and Jonson, especially the last, help Carew to celebrate the good life, Classical style, and its values of friendship and hospitality. In his poems praising Saxham and Wrest, Carew reveals his intimate friendships with the great families of the day and opens up vignettes (somewhat "Classicalized") of his period's social customs, architecture, gardens, and vegetable and animal life.

Little Saxham in Suffolk was the family seat of the Crofts, a family whose members were complimented in several poems of Carew. John Crofts had become Carew's friend probably during their service with Sir Edward Herbert in France.

The frost and snow of winter block from the poet's eyes the outdoors beauty on this visit "To Saxham" (27 - 29), but inside is so pleasant that "neither from, nor to thy store / Winter takes ought, or Spring addes more" (ll. 9 - 10). And the poor are preserved from the destruction of winter by Saxham's bounty. Carew plays, like Jonson in "To Penshurst," on the gratitude and willing sacrifice of the creatures who surround Saxham, bringing biblical overtones to support his case and "Classicizing" with "scalie herd" (l. 27) in the manner of Milton and his eighteenth-century imitators:

> The season hardly did afford
> Course cates unto thy neighbours board,
> Yet thou hadst daintyes, as the skie
> Had only been thy Volarie;
> Or else the birds, fearing the snow
> Might to another deluge grow:
> The Pheasant, Partiridge, and the Larke,
> Flew to thy house, as to the Arke.
> The willing Oxe, of himselfe came
> Home to the slaughter, with the Lambe,
> And every beast did thither bring
> Himselfe, to be an offering.

> The scalie herd, more pleasure tooke,
> Bath'd in thy dish, then in the brooke. . . .[9]
>
> (ll. 15 - 28)

Not only do the creatures come to Saxham as to the ark, but there is an echo of its being so peaceful that "the lion will lie down with the lamb." The peace of this great estate is well supported by the smooth and supple tetrameter couplets.

As the "pregnant fire" of Henrietta Maria inspired the other three elements in "To the Queene" (90 - 91), so here the (hearth) fire is paid tribute by water, earth, and air. It divides in every room to form "suns within" and "keepe endlesse day" (l. 34), staging a welcome for pilgrims. This emblem of bounty faithfully symbolizes the hospitality of master and of "hinde," molded in his master's image. No one outstays his welcome or finds what he has to eat and drink measured. There are no locks or bolts, the gates themselves having been made "onely to let strangers in" (l. 52). No fears rule in this country house: "And as for theeves, thy bountie's such, / They cannot steale, thou giv'st so much" (ll. 57 - 58). One misses Jonson's "ripe daughters" "whose baskets bear / An emblem of themselves in plum or pear" ("To Penshurst," ll. 54 - 56), but gains, despite the absence of people, in subtle portrayal of the genial liberality of a house where no room has to be shut off to conserve heat.

"To the King at his entrance into Saxham, by Master Jo. Crofts" (30 - 31) forms a kind of companion piece to the poem above. It was probably written by Carew and recited by John Crofts during a royal visit in February 1619 / 20. The device chosen is to celebrate the King (in tetrameter couplets) with rites that would ordinarily be performed to the Classical household gods. The result is more inventive than efficacious.

The altar of sacrifice is displaced by the "flaming Altar" (l. 6) of each greeter's breast. Incense becomes thankfulness. The "slaughter'd beast" (l. 15) is dressed for the King's supper, and the blood that would be dashed on doors (a biblical sacrificial image) is transformed into wine. After "homely cheare" (l. 27), there may be a "countrie dance." To amend the celebrants' efforts, King James must lay aside his greatness and allow only mercy. Despite their faults, however, they swear "Should *Jove* descend, they could no more" (ll. 45 - 46).

Another great country estate frequented by Carew is extolled in "To my friend G. N. from Wrest" (86 - 89), perhaps Carew's last poem since it alludes in the opening to the difficult conditions endured by those in attendance upon Charles in his expedition against Scotland during the spring of 1639. "G. N." ("Ghib" in the poem) has not been certainly identified, though Wrest Park is the manor house of the De Greys in Bedfordshire. Carew's poem seems to be most influenced by Jonson's "To Sir Robert Wroth."

Again in rhyming pentameter couplets (but with a final hexameter couplet by catalexis), Carew is pleased to be away from the "wilde North" and at Wrest, where, in a classic image,

> . . . the pregnant Earth
> Sends from her teeming wombe a flowrie birth,
> And cherisht with the warme Suns quickning heate,
> Her porous bosome doth rich odours sweate;
> Whose perfumes through the Ambient ayre diffuse
> Such native Aromatiques, as we use
> No forraigne Gums, nor essence fetcht from farre,
> No Volatile spirits, nor compounds that are
> Adulterate, but at Natures cheape expence
> With farre more genuine sweetes refresh the sense.
> (ll. 9 - 18)

The personification of Earth with her "porous bosome" sweating "rich odours" serves notice that Carew, as he goes on to claim, will allow no lifelessness about Wrest any more than Nature herself will permit adulterated and artificial scents here. The same demand for naturalness is next praised in the house itself, "Devoide of Art" (l. 21) and built "for hospitalitie" (l. 24), motives that would delight a modern architect and that were of course in frequent discussion in the seventeenth century. Instead of with statues, as one might expect, the house is filled with "living men" (l. 34), who are seated in the "merry Hall" (l. 34) with all respect for rank and privilege duly observed. The "streightned" exterior portends no dearth within:

> . . . *Amalthea's* Horne
> Of plentie is not in Effigie worne
> Without the gate, but she within the dore
> Empties her free and unexhausted store.
> (ll. 57 - 60)

Ceres and Bacchus are likewise no mere statues here but real bread and wine, respectively.

Lest Wrest be felt devoid of Art, however, Carew points out that she becomes handmaiden to Nature to produce, with implicit patriotism, another "precious stone set in the silver sea," an England in miniature:

> Yet we decline not, all the worke of Art,
> But where more bounteous Nature beares a part
> And guides her Hand-maid, if she but dispence
> Fit matter, she with care and diligence
> Employes her skill, for where the neighbour sourse
> Powers forth her waters she directs their course,
> And entertaines the flowing streames in deepe
> And spacious channells, where they slowly creepe
> In snakie windings, as the shelving ground
> Leades them in circles, till they twice surround
> This Island Mansion, which i' th' center plac'd,
> Is with a double Crystall heaven embrac'd,
> In which our watery constellations floate,
> Our Fishes, Swans, our Water-man and Boate,
> Envy'd by those above, which wish to slake
> Their starre-burnt limbes, in our refreshing lake
> But they stick fast nayl'd to the barren Spheare,
> Whilst our encrease in fertile waters here
> Disport, and wander freely where they please
> Within the circuit of our narrow Seas.
>   (ll. 69 - 88)[10]

The desire of the stars and constellations to refresh themselves in Wrest's lake may take the poem into hyperbole by constrasting the estate favorably with heaven, but it also subtly proclaims the order inherent in the Great Chain of Being. The necessity for order is what partially drew the Renaissance to the Classical period in the first place. Jonson especially praised in his country-house poems the aristocratic harmony that saw each person and each creature and object in its particular place. Carew has reproduced this feeling in the decorous relationships among all parts of the natural world of Wrest where, even in man-made areas, Nature and Art are not forced into competition. Now Carew draws on the old microcosm-macrocosm linking but plays on it wittily by having Wrest *entice* heaven rather than simply reflect its accord and peacefulness.

Nature and Art and heaven and earth continue to mingle as Wrest's grounds become the haunt of Vertumnus and Pomona, Zephyr and Flora, and Bacchus and Ceres. It is a place of "blest

Peace" (l. 108) where the only "memory of our Armes" (l. 110) is to be found in "Ghib's" hunting of the buck and the stag.

IV *Engagements and Marriages*

A group of slight poems, adhering to the genre of the epithalamion or marriage poem, depicts once more Carew's attentiveness to events among the nobility. Perhaps the cleverest, also in pentameter couplets, is "On the Marriage of T. K. [Thomas Killigrew] and C. C. [Cecilia Crofts] the morning stormie" (79 - 80), the pair for whom Carew's "Jealousie" (59 - 60) was supposedly written.

The task set the poet is very believable and would of course have been difficult. He must convince the lady that a stormy wedding morn prognosticates no ill future. Rather, in a gracious compliment, the sun is said to be "bashful," unwilling to risk his brightness in competition with hers, though he cannot forbear squinting occasionally through the clouds to see her glories. Moreover, the tears and sighs of the unrequited suitor have now been turned over to the clouds and wind, his "blubbred eyes" (l. 16, an image used a number of times by Carew) having been dried by the approaching marriage. The lowering heavens and stormy gusts emblematize the bridegroom's toilsome courtship. If he recalls its hardships, the "fight of love" (l. 31) upcoming will be enjoyed the more for the contrast. Indeed, Carew, pursuing this line of thought, seems to forget that a *lady* needs reassurance:

> Then boldly to the fight of Love proceed,
> 'Tis mercy not to pitty though she bleed,
> Wee'le strew no nuts, but change that ancient forme,
> For till to morrow wee'le prorogue this storme,
> Which shall confound with its loude whistling noyse
> Her pleasing shreekes, and fan thy panting joyes.
> (ll. 31 - 36)

The poem is a tour de force from the graceful compliments to the bride to the final leverage Carew gets from the storm as it increases the groom's sexual appetite and drowns out her "pleasing shreekes" as her maidenhead is reaped. Though there is basically nothing about the poem that is new, Carew reveals in it his capacity to absorb and enliven his borrowings. It is one of his best renderings of the unembarrassed joys of sexuality; one wonders if the fact that he is talking about *married* love has made the difference, no matter how blasé Carew often seems to be.

More restrained is "An Hymeneall Song on the Nuptials of the Lady *Ann Wentworth,* and the Lord *Lovelace*" (114 - 15), another poem on the Crofts family, for Lady Ann's mother was John Crofts's sister. As the poem opens, the bride is sleeping on the morning of the wedding; and Carew uses the same conceit for her brightness as for that of Cecilia Crofts. When she awakens, the sun must "give place." She needs her sleep, however, for tonight she must keep "An Amarous Vigill" (l. 8). Yet she must be gently wakened to make her procession to temple and feast, "Then back to bed, though not to rest" (l. 18). Lord Lovelace has triumphed and must now revel in Love's sphere as its chief intelligence:

> They know no night, nor glaring noone,
> Measure no houres of Sunne or Moone,
>   Nor mark times restlesse Glasse:
>
> Their kisses measure as they flow,
> Minutes, and their embraces show
>   The howers [with a pun on "ours"] as they passe.
>
> Their Motions, the yeares Circle make,
> And we from their conjunctions take
> Rules to make Love an Almanack.
>   (ll. 28 - 36)[11]

Subtly, Carew suggests that this pair has mastered Time by loving and marrying and that now they control him, a witty play on the *carpe diem* topos.

The most unusual features of this poem, however, are the rhyme scheme of the tercets and the complex variation in line length. The twelve stanzas form three metrical groups, the first group rhyming aab ccb ddd. The first and second stanzas follow two lines of iambic tetrameter with a line of iambic trimeter. The third stanza consists of three lines of iambic tetrameter. The remaining two groups follow the same form. This is the most complicated scheme Carew has used when working with tercets and in fact matches his metrical complexity anywhere else.

The marriage of Carew's distant relation Carew Raleigh (the son of Sir Walter Raleigh) and the widow Phillippa Ashley is rather formally saluted in "To my Cousin (C. R.) marrying my Lady (A.)" (47). Carew had visited the Carew Raleigh manor house (West Horsley), too, and had corresponded with his friend Sir John Suckling while there. Curiously, he suggests that the bridegroom, the

"Happy Youth," will possess "Such a spring-tyde of delight" as will make him "Wish the flood of pleasure lesse" (ll. 1 - 5) and that he must invoke night to dress his "too reall happinesse" in shadows:

> Else (as *Semele*) the bright
> Deitie in her full might,
> May thy feeble soule oppresse.
> (ll. 10 - 12)

Then another proverbial (and rather offensive this time) final couplet: "Stong perfumes, and glaring light, / Oft destroy both smell, and sight" (ll. 13 - 14). It is strange that in some of his amorous lyrics to women not his wife, Carew tries to Platonize the erotic while in most of his celebrations of marriage, he blatantly declares for sexual fulfillment. Again, one cannot too quickly pass him off as a merely erotic poet. Nor, as the same poem testifies, can he be dismissed as an always regular follower of Jonson's smooth ways. "To my Cousin . . ." is another poem in which Carew makes free use of catalectic lines (all are catalectic) and an unusual rhyme scheme (abbaabbabbabb). Stranger is the fact that, despite the look of the foreshortened lines, they too are tetrameters, but trochaic this time.

Still more formal verses compliment Sir John Finch's choice in "Upon my Lord Chief Justice his election of my Lady A. W. for his Mistresse" (83 - 84), the same Anne Wentworth whose marriage to Lord Lovelace was later versified by Carew. Its four stanzas (ababccc) are distinguished by the variation among trimeter, tetrameter, dimeter, and pentameter lines and by the maintenance of legal images in keeping with the position of Finch.

The Golden Age has returned and with it the Goddess of Justice:

> *Astraea* hath possest
> An earthly seate, and now remaines
> In *Finches* heart, but *Wentworths* brest
> That Guest containes;
> With her she dwells, yet hath not left the skies,
> Nor lost her Spheare, for, new-enthron'd she cryes
> I know no Heaven but fayre *Wentworths* eyes.
> (ll. 22 - 28)[12]

The new regime will operate by the banishment of Cupid and all of his paraphernalia, as Carew (though decorously) fits his narrative to his subjects. Still, the poem remains a light bit of wit with little substance. The close development of a single idea is present, but the poet does not convince the reader of his own involvement with this particular "game of love."

V *On Holidays and in Times of Sickness*

Carew bids New Year's greetings in three poems, two addressed to "Lucinda," Lucy, the Countess of Carlisle, a lady ensconced in many poems of the day and linked again with Carew in Suckling's dialogue, "Upon my Lady Carliles walking in Hampton-Court garden," in which he and Carew discuss her "powers." Carew's "A New-yeares Sacrifice. To Lucinda" (32 - 33),[13] probably written in 1633 and in pentameter couplets, rejects the "cheape and vulgar wishes" (l. 9) for her invoked by others and declares it "Apostasy" (l. 11) to send a prayer to any deity but her. The whole is centered on the conceit of the poet come to worship at the "goddess'" shrine. The earlier[14] "To the New-yeare, for the Countesse of Carlile" (91 - 92), done in tetrameter tercets (aaa, with all the lines truncated), applies more traditional compliments. Lucinda needs no gems, for "Her beautie shine[s] alone" (l. 3). Nor does she need spice or gum, for the phoenix nests in her breasts and gives off wondrous odors, and so on. Both poems end in confirmation that she can inspire more poetry.

"A New-yeares gift. To the King" (89 - 90) also alludes to Janus, as would be expected, and more extensively and effectually than "To the New-yeare, for the Countesse of Carlile." Janus is requested to look backward into the old year, gather all its "Happie auspitious dayes" (l. 6), and wreathe from them a crown for Charles "That we th' ensuing yeare may call / One great continued festivall" (ll. 13 - 14). For the King himself, the poet makes this request: let him be happy as husband, father, and ruler of a land of peace. Carew's skill as a poet greatly surpasses his powers as a prophet, for "Byfront" is requested to "open thou no more, / In his blest raigne the Temple dore" (ll. 33 - 34), playing on the tradition that the doors of Janus's temple were closed only during times of peace. The chauvinism of the Cavalier is as rampant in these tetrameter couplets as in "In answer of an Elegiacall Letter upon the death of the King of Sweden from Aurelian Townsend, inviting me to write on that subject"(74 - 77).

The pentameter couplets of "Upon the Kings sicknesse" (35 - 36) express the same commitment to the Monarch shared by all the

Cavaliers, though the figure in question is probably not Charles but James I in his last illness of 1625. Using the image of the "besieged fort," usually applied to love, Carew tells of the encroachment of Death upon mankind from cradle to manhood. The King's illness indicates that no longer will Death be slowed:

> Thus by degrees it onely gain'd of late,
> The weake, the aged, or intemperate;
> But now the Tyrant hath found out a way
> By which the sober, strong, and young, decay. . . .
> (ll. 15 - 18)[15]

With the attack on the King, all of his subjects are besieged.

Another image Carew has customarily used for love, as in "Celia bleeding, to the Surgeon" (26), is adapted: "Through us his mystique limbe the paine is spread" (l. 20), a reworking of an idea in King James's own *The True Law of Free Monarchies*. The court feels this grief that is felt even more by that "ruddie morning beame of Majestie" (l. 29), apparently Prince Charles. Almost as if he were conscious that "the King *is dying*, long live the King," Carew devotes twelve lines to Charles:

> That ruddie morning beame of Majestie,
> Which should the Suns ecclipsed light supply,
> Is overcast with mists, and in the liew
> Of cherefull rayes, sends us downe drops of dew:
> That curious forme made of an earth refin'd,
> At whose blest birth, the gentle Planets shin'd
> With faire aspects, and sent a glorious flame
> To animate so beautifull a frame;
> That Darling of the Gods and men, doth weare
> A cloude on's brow, and in his eye a teare:
> And all the rest, (save when his dread command
> Doth bid them move,) like livelesse statues stand. . . .
> (ll. 29 - 40)

Carew returns to the true subject only in the final pointed couplet: "So full a griefe, so generally worne / Shewes a good King is sick, and good men mourne" (ll. 41 - 42). As usual when Carew is writing hyperbolical commendation, there is little to admire with the possible exception of the extended treatment of Prince Charles as the "sun."

Three remaining poems on the sicknesses of his friends and acquaintances are far less serious. The two companion-poems, "On
Mistris N. to the greene sicknesse" (113) and "To M^ris Katherine
Nevill on her greene sicknesse" (129), both in tetrameter couplets,
are probably addressed to the sisters Mary and Katherine Neville.
Both play on the paleness attentive upon this anemic disease, and
the former cleverly adapts it for the struggle between the traditional
white and red of the sonnet lady's complexion:

> Stay coward blood, and doe not yield
> To thy pale sister, beauties field,
> Who there displaying round her white
> Ensignes, hath usurp'd thy right;
> Invading thy peculiar throne,
> The lip, where thou shouldst rule alone;
> And on the cheeke, where natures care
> Allotted each an equall share,
> Her spreading Lilly only growes,
> Whose milky deluge drownes thy Rose.
> (ll. 1 - 10)

The second verse paragraph employs martial imagery, also from
sonnet lore; but the "war" is not here between male and female but
between the colors that should have equal shares in the lady's
cheek. Again it is Carew's adaptation of borrowed materials that
gives the poem the small success of wit that it possesses.

In the second poem (129), the white of the ill young lady's cheeks
has been forsaken ("widdowed," l. 2) by the red. Various expedients
are to be tried to recall it; and, when it returns, the poet will cut off
any further retreats. White, red, and the poet-lover will then have
their proper shares:

> O lodge me there, where Ile defeate
> All future hope of his retreate,
> And force the fugitive to seeke
> A constant station in thy cheeke.
> Soe each shall have his proper place,
> I in your heart, he in your face.
> (ll. 13 - 18)

Carew conveys the impression that no matter how many Neville
sisters there might be, he could manage to provide poetic variations
on the same basic materials. It is seldom that his ingenuity lies dor-
mant.

Whatever the disease in "Upon the sicknesse of (E. S.)" (31 - 32), perhaps Elizabeth Sheldon, later the Countess of Anglesey, it too works a paleness, making the poet exclaim that Justice must now have fled from heaven as well. What else can account for the fact that a "foule deformed ravisher" is allowed to sit "Upon her Virgin cheek, and pull from thence / The Rose-buds in their maiden excellence" (ll. 4 - 6), frighten away her "Rubies" (l. 8), and "lick up with his searching flames, a flood / Of dissolv'd Corall, flowing in her blood" (ll. 9 - 10)? In these pentameter couplets, Diana cannot dare allow agues and diseases to embrace this chaste lady whom "Princes have desir'd to taste" (l. 17). Apollo and Cupid are also urged to be in attendance; and Venus, the poet imagines, will (with the usual "pearls" and "hairie Coronet") be her handmaiden and minister to her needs, keeping her safe from "chilling cold, or burning Calenture" (l. 42) unless they represent the ice of chastity or the fires of Hymen. Thus when Death comes, Cupid will give him his "golden" dart of love, the only kind of "killing" allowable for one so protected: "And when at last Death comes to pierce her heart, / Convey into his hand thy golden dart" (ll. 45 - 46).

This poem, like a few others of Carew, falls from its opening into overwrought hyperbole and ingenuity. Even so and despite the derived images, Carew can produce a moment of some beauty. For example, once past E. S.'s "balmie sweat" as perfume (ll. 35 - 36), the reader finds the drops of sweat hanging in the hair "like rich Pearles about a wreath of gold" (l. 38), an image also not new but which Carew made distinctively his own.

VI *Elegies and Obsequies*

It would be odd if Carew had not contributed to the popular seventeenth-century genre of funereal poetry; and the poems of this group, especially those on Mary Villiers and Maria Wentworth, were well known among his early critics. They form an important segment of Carew's poetry, including, of course, "An Elegie upon the death of the Deane of Pauls, Dr. John Donne," "Obsequies to the Lady Anne Hay," and "An Elegie on the La: Pen: sent to my Mistresse out of France," all discussed earlier.

If "E. S." in the poem above is Elizabeth Sheldon, she is also addressed in "To the Countesse of Anglesie upon the immoderatly-by-her-lamented death of her Husband" (69 - 71), where Carew indicates his role in her courtship by Christopher Villiers, brother of the Duke of Buckingham ("When I his sighes to you, and back your teares / Convay'd to him . . . ," ll. 72 - 73). The elegy is immediately "odd" by embedding its lamentation for the count (ll. 27 - 78) within the frame of an address to the mourning wife intended to allay grief. Like the elegy on Donne, this poem is a verse-epistle in run-on pentameter couplets forming "paragraphs," though it is the widow rather than the deceased who is addressed.

A clever conceit opens the argument as Carew reports that "men say" her tears water "the Rose that lyes / Fall'n from your cheeks upon your deare Lords Hearse" (ll. 1 - 3). Unfortunately, this "flood of pearly moysture" lacks the virtues "fabled of old *AEsons* bath" (ll. 7 - 8), an alchemical image. She may through her grief bring an autumn upon herself "but not call back his spring" (ll. 13 - 14). Obtrusive woe is, she must be made to see, a "vulgar trade" (l. 19) and is not needed to show her love whose "every act crown'd you a constant Wife" (l. 18). Rather, she should now become the pattern of the wise widow as formerly she was of the wise wife.

Yet, to explain to "the world" why she has cause to grieve, he moves into the elegy proper, the eulogy of Lord Villiers, eulogy being standard fare in contemporary elegies. The quaintest thought in this eulogy is that the count

> . . . was compos'd of all
> The wishes of ripe Virgins, when they call
> For Hymens rites, and in their fancies wed
> A shape of studied beauties to their bed.
> (ll. 37 - 40)

Thereafter, Villiers is treated with almost Classical formality, becoming the very exemplar of the Horatian retreat topos usually reserved for the country-house poems:

> He chose not in the active streame to swim,
> Nor hunted Honour; which, yet hunted him.
> But like a quiet Eddie, that hath found
> Some hollow creeke, there turnes his waters round,
> And in continuall circles, dances free
> From the impetuous Torrent; so did hee
> Give others leave to turne the wheele of State,
> *(Whose restlesse motion spins the subjects fate)*
> Whilst he retir'd from the tumultuous noyse
> Of Court, and suitors presse; apart, enjoyes
> Freedome, and mirth, himselfe, his time, and friends,
> And with sweet rellish tastes each houre he spends.
> (ll. 57 - 68)

This passage also shows once again Carew's versatility, for he has taken two images, personified Honor and the quiet eddy, usually applied in love poems, and turned them into commendations of Lord Villiers. At the last, Carew reminds the wife of her husband's fidelity under the disguise of fearing to mention it lest he awaken new grief.

The return from eulogizing the husband to comforting the widow is effected by requesting that she look to her husband's "bright flame," mingled with that of his dead brother, the Duke of Buckingham, and "derive a chearfull influence." Thus in time to come, the poet can turn his pen from elegy to "the Trophies of your conquering eye" (ll. 79 - 86). This preparation for going on with her life now that the lady's husband is dead, to the point of suggesting that she will have other admirers, is akin to the note that emerges in some of Carew's love lyrics (e.g., "Oh love me then, and now begin it," in "To A. L. Perswasions to love").

Two elegies, both in tetrameter couplets (except for the shift to pentameters in the final couplet of the second), are reserved for the Duke of Buckingham himself, a well-known figure at the courts of both James and Charles, who was murdered by John Felton on August 23, 1628. "On the Duke of Buckingham" (57) anticipates that Fame will declare this "fair / Structure" ("by the studious care / Of two Kings rays'd") the victim of "blinded zeale" (ll. 1 - 9). The annals can record his actions. Here there is room only for the obsequies of his wife's tears, which, in a standard image, used, for example, by Marvell in "The Nymph complaining for the death of her Faun," carve his monument:

> These are the pious Obsequies,
> Drop'd from his chast Wifes pregnant eyes
> In frequent showres, and were alone
> By her congealing sighes made stone,
> On which the Carver did bestow
> These formes and characters of woe;
> So he the fashion onely lent,
> Whilst she wept all this Monument.
>   (ll. 25 - 32)

All in all, it is one of the least impressive of Carew's elegies.

"An other" (58) adopts a favorite device of funereal poetry in addressing the "reader" with the age-old adage that the "vaine" pursuit "Of humane Glory yeelds no fruit, / But an untimely Grave" (ll. 3 - 5). The middle portion eulogizes Villiers (in very general terms) under the ploy of proving that the best must die:

> Safe in the circle of his Friends:
> Safe in his Loyall heart, and ends:
> Safe in his native valiant spirit:
> By favour safe, and safe by merit;
> Safe by the stampe of Nature, which
> Did strength, with shape and Grace enrich:
> Safe in the cheerefull Curtesies
> Of flowing gestures, speach, and eyes:
> Safe in his Bounties, which were more
> Proportion'd to his mind then store;
> Yet, though for vertue he becomes
> Involv'd Himselfe in borrowed summes,
> Safe in his care, he leaves betray'd
> No friend engag'd, no debt unpay'd.
>   (ll. 13 - 26)

The use of repetition and variation ("Safe. . . .") is a new approach for Carew and one of the most successful devices of the poem. The next conceit is less original: the stars have showered all their graces upon Buckingham, but their dire aspects upon his assassin. The enigmatical final couplet (shifting from tetrameter to pentameter) thus is phrased as a question: "Who can be happy then, if Nature must / To make one Happy man, make all men just?" (ll. 33 - 34).

Among Carew's most cleverly fashioned and "gem"-ridden poems in this class is the "Epitaph on the Lady S. [Mary, the wife of Sir William Salter] Wife to Sir W. S." (55), for it aligns the standard "language of gems" with biblical allusions:

> . . . Shee was a Cabinet
> Where all the choysest stones of price were set;
>
> . . .
>
> The constant Diamond, the wise Chrysolite,
> The devout Saphyre, Emrauld apt to write
> Records of Memory, cheerefull Agat, grave
> And serious Onyx, Tophaze, that doth save
> The braines calme temper, witty Amathist.
> This precious Quarrie, or what else the list
> On *Aarons* Ephod planted, had, shee wore:

> One only Pearle was wanting to her store,
> Which in her Saviours booke she found exprest,
> To purchase that, she sold Death all the rest.
> (ll. 5 - 6, 11 - 20)

Once again, Carew brings in the lapidary imagery of the jewel cabinet as Lady Salter's virtues, physical and spiritual, are paraded through the stones found therein. She contained all of the jewels of Aaron's ephod (Exodus 28: 4 - 39) save one, the "pearl of great price" (Matthew 13: 45 - 46); and, to obtain that, she has willingly bargained with Death. The poem demonstrates what is seldom recognized about Carew's poetry: a persisting strain of biblical imagery. He knows the Bible well enough to heighten his subjects with it and well enough, at other times, to parody it. Here the biblical allusions are the most outstanding feature of this poem in smooth pentameter couplets.

Aside from the tribute to John Donne, the best-known (and the most Jonsonian[16]) elegies of Carew are the three on Mary Villiers (possibly the daughter of the Earl and Countess of Anglesey, though the implication of the first that the child's father was still alive makes this identification suspect) and the one on Maria Wentworth. The first three are as simple and moving as Jonson's on Solomon Pavy and his own children, the lines seeming shorter (despite the fact that they are all iambic tetrameter) and the couplets crisper than is Carew's habit.

The "Epitaph on the Lady Mary Villers" (53 - 54) begins with four factual lines stating the case. The child's parents and their friends buried her "Under this stone." The reader is then requested to "shed a teare" if he knows any of these parties or if he has a "gemme"—Carew resorts to one of his favorite images and perhaps thinks again of the "pearl of great price"—as dear (ll. 5 - 8). The last four lines sound, in the notes of the Classical *consolatio* or consolation tradition, the mortality of all mankind:

> Though a stranger to this place,
> Bewayle in theirs, thine owne hard case;
> For thou perhaps at thy returne
> Mayest find thy Darling in an Urne.
> (ll. 9 - 12)

Carew has fully captured the terse style of Greek epitaphs. Henry Headley, with some justification, considers this "Carew's masterpiece."[17] The truncated lines (6 and 9) reinforce the feeling of especial grief for the wrenching away of a child.

The other two, because their verse is totally regular and because their images are more contrived, are less appealing. The first (54) decorously, however, employs a figure for Love, the cherubic child of Venus, which complements the child-subject of the poem:

> Ten thousand *Cupids* brought along
> A Grace on each wing, that did throng
> For plaoe there, till they all opprest
> The seat in which they sought to rest;
> So the faire Modell broke, for want
> Of roome to lodge th' Inhabitant.
>   (ll. 7 - 12)

It can be argued that the child "purifies" the Venerian tradition to suggest cherubim and a Christian rather than a merely Classical "grace." As preparation for these thronging Cupids, each pushing to bring graces to Mary Villiers, Carew has reinstituted the old conceit, to be found again in his treatment of Maria Wentworth, that the "weake mold" of the body could not contain that purest substance, her soul. So concentrated is the poem that Rufus Blanshard uses it to illustrate "the most important distinguishing feature of Carew's power," developing "a single image or a cluster of images."[18]

The final and longest of the three Mary Villiers elegies (54, bottom) relates this "bud," who "yet did containe / More sweetnesse then shall spring again," "this budding starre that might have growne / Into a Sun," to Love, surely for the modern sensibility, a curious juxtaposition. It uses a crescendo of images ("dawning beame," "bud," "budding starre," "hopefull beautie") to establish the inroad the child was making to Love (ll. 1 - 11). The "new life" she breathed into "Loves declining state" ended with her (ll. 11 - 12), but paradoxically (with borrowings from Ronsard) she wrought nonetheless a transformation of the erotic Cupid, the implication is, into the cherubic figure of the previous poem. As a result,

> . . . we
> From fire, and wounding darts are free:
> His brand, his bow, let no man feare,
> The flames, the arrowes, all lye here.
>   (ll. 13 - 16)

The more Carew draws on conventional imagery—no matter how well he may convert images of love to the rites of death—the less sincere he seems in the elegies.

It is fitting to close the discussion of Carew's poems with the epitaph on Maria Wentworth (56), in tercets (aaa), for it is generally considered to display, perhaps at its best, Carew's distinctive combination of Metaphysical and Jonsonian influences and to anticipate the Augustan spirit that was to prevail in English poetry. When F. R. Leavis "revaluated" "Carew and the Line of Wit," he found Stanzas 4 and 5 Augustan, with the effect of the whole being quite different. Opening in the manner of Jonson's epitaphs, the poem turns, Leavis said, to a conceit (the soul breaking the shell / body of sin and hatching into a cherub) in the mode of Jonson and Donne. The third stanza he interpreted as Metaphysical, with "Caroline wit" reasserted in the "chaste Poligamie" of Stanza 6, and the final lines displaying Marvellian movement.[19] Here is the poem:

> And here the precious dust is layd;
> Whose purely-tempered Clay was made
> So fine, that it the guest betray'd.
>
> Else the soule grew so fast within,
> It broke the outward shell of sinne,
> And so was hatch'd a Cherubin.
>
> In heigth, it soar'd to God above;
> In depth, it did to knowledge move,
> And spread in breadth to generall love.
>
> Before, a pious duty shind
> To Parents, courtesie behind,
> On either side an equall mind,
>
> Good to the Poore, to kindred deare,
> To servants kind, to friendship cleare,
> To nothing but her selfe, severe.
>
> So though a Virgin, yet a Bride
> To every Grace, she justifi'd
> A chaste Poligamie, and dy'd.
>
> Learne from hence (Reader) what small trust
> We owe this world, where vertue must
> Fraile as our flesh, crumble to dust.

Maria, who died in January 1632 / 33, was the daughter of Sir Thomas Wentworth. Her tomb, in the Church of St. George, Toddington, Bedfordshire, is inscribed with a version of Carew s first six stanzas and shows her seated, her sewing basket in her hands. (The local legend runs that she died from a prick of her finger while she was sewing on a Sunday.) She is another member of the Crofts family.

Eighteen when she died and thus presumably older than Mary Villiers, she is accorded in general a different set of accolades, though the poem begins with the same conceit of the disparity between flesh and spirit used in the second epitaph on the Villiers child, expanded here into the soul's transformation into the cherub. What has not been pointed out by critics is the wit of the three central stanzas, which reaffirm the spirit-body division of the first two. In every direction (height, depth, breadth; before, behind, on either side), she was spirit first; to everyone (the poor, servants, her kindred, her friends) but herself, she was spirit first. Little wonder, then, that she soon "soar'd to God above," where in the most controversial image of this poetically regular poem,[20] she, like the virgins of Revelation who became the Brides of the Lamb (Christ), can be "though a Virgin, yet a Bride" and know a "chaste Poligamie." The poem, after this startling revelation, concludes in the manner of another Greek epitaph, admonishing the "reader," as in the "Epitaph on the Lady Mary Villers," to take heed, for, in this untrustworthy world, "vertue must / Fraile as our flesh, crumble to dust."

CHAPTER 6

Coelum Britannicum

S INCE Carew was so closely connected with the English court and with the kind of poetry favored by the court, it is odd that he did not write more of the great symbolic court entertainments of the period, the masque. His one work in the genre, *Coelum Britannicum*, proves that he had studied the form closely.

Probably of Italian origin, the masque received its greatest development at the hands of Ben Jonson during the Jacobean and Caroline periods. As was the case with his country-house poems, Jonson's masques were intended to demonstrate the moral motives of poetry. Not only were the masquers members of the courtly audience, but their symbolic costumes, the mythological themes and stage sets used in the masques, and their dancing and music taught the spectators and the participants themselves lessons in order and harmony. Those great lessons were most in evidence at the climax when the members of the audience joined the masquers in the final dance, a tacit acknowledgment that *all* present accepted and understood the reassertion of order and decorum.

Jonson himself inaugurated and developed the antimasque ("antic-" or "anti-" masque), which he used as a prelude or interlude not only to provide dramatic contrast, but to show the dangers of disruptions of order. On one level, the whole masque was a war between the personified vices (of the antimasque) and virtues. In the masque the (aristocratic) virtues always triumphed.

Under James I, Jonson's masques prospered, for the King shared the poet's interest in the messages of the poetry. Charles I, on the other hand, favored the great "spectacle" of the masque, its lavish sets and stage machinery, the latter exchanging one world for another in the flash of an eye. Charles's Queen, Henrietta Maria, poured out great sums on these entertainments. The result was that Inigo Jones, the famous architect who had collaborated with Jonson on many masques, achieved the ascendancy, and Jonson began to lose his place at court.

Inigo Jones helped Carew with *Coelum Britannicum*. As one would immediately conclude, spectacle is therefore of central importance in Carew's masque. Even so, there is at least a conventional seriousness of political theme about it, as the title indicates with its intention of showing the heaven that is Britain.

I *Summary*

The "ornament" enclosing the scene is decorated with foliage, harpies, and heads of children and is inscribed with the name of Carew's masque, *Coelum Britannicum*. From one side a golden vase rises supported by two naked youths sitting at its base. Two young women stand on the cover to represent the glory of princes and their mansuetude and to bear the impress of Charles I. The other side is similarly adorned and bears the impress of Queen Henrietta Maria.

The curtain suddenly is raised upon a scene of decaying arches, broken walls, and the ruins of some Roman city. To loud music, Mercury descends in his chariot, which also contains a crowing cock. He has a feathered hat, wings on his heels, and a caduceus. He dismounts and approaches the throne of the King and Queen, announcing that he is Jove's ambassador, not come, as formerly, to whisper amorous tales but to announce the Reformation in heaven proclaimed by Jove as a result of their majesties' exemplary lives. Jealous Juno has in the past been preoccupied with transforming Jove's paramours into beasts. In sorrow, Jove stellified them or changed them into stars so that the heavens have been filled with "loose strumpets." Great Jove now determines to banish these and replace them with the British King and Queen.

Momus enters with his "particolored" beard and hair and his porcupine quills. Since the poets never have called him from heaven, he has come on his own to prove his worth and thus proceeds to give an account of himself. Mercury is impatient to know what all this has to do with Jove; but Momus insists that, as a free-born god, he can tell this "trimme audience" about heaven. As he begins his recital, a virtual "popularized" version of Mercury's opening address, the scene changes to depict in the heavens the sphere of stars with Atlas bearing its weight on his shoulders. Momus reports in skeptical terms the proclamations issued to carry out Jove's Reformation, concluding his "blunt round tale" with an account of heaven's conjugal changes, illustrated most directly by the inscription of "Carlomaria" (a blending of King Charles and Queen

Henrietta Maria) engraved on the bedchamber door of Jove and Juno.

Momus next invites Mercury to complete his task by calling to account the inhabitants of the eighth sphere, who are already hanging loose in their sockets. Mercury obliges, waves his caduceus, and purges the heavens of the constellations, calling forth the denizens to deliver the first antimasque, of "natural depravity," after which they are banished to "Fens, Caves, Forrests, Deserts, Seas." Among the signs of the zodiac, the crab is singled out for especial condemnation; and the second antimasque mirrors his disorders "in retrograde paces, expressing obliquity in motion."

Mercury describes the encroachments of Vice upon the heavens (e.g., flattery in the "little Dog," "Ambition in the Eagle") and summons the third antimasque, a dance "of these severall vices, expressing the deviation from Vertue." Now Momus begins to worry about the security of the earth if such are to be let loose here; they would be less dangerous, he maintains, nailed as usual to the firmament or sent to New England! Mercury rejoinders that they will be unable to endure "this pure and temperate Aire / Where Vertue lives" and will flee to "fogs and vapours" (ll. 392 - 94) of their own accord. He banishes the remaining stars; and the eighth sphere, having been progressively emptied at each conjuration by Mercury, is now totally dark. Momus feels that some might have been saved; and he moves quickly to proclaim a new succession there and calls for those of transcendent virtue to plead their cause and remove to the seat of the stars, if they are found worthy.

The first to assert his rights is Plutus, who declares that Virtue is his slave and that he "lead[s] her captive in a golden chaine, / About the world" (ll. 490 - 91). Men forsake the other gods for him, thus showing his power "Too great for Earth, and onely fit for Heaven" (l. 528). To cap his argument, he presents as the fourth antimasque "Countrey people, musique and measures." Mercury admits his power, but banishes Plutus, who has caused the plagues of "lust for empire," to follow war camps and be the slave of conquerors.

Poenia or Poverty claims heaven with the false logic (decried by Momus) that her foe and opposite, Plutus, being denied access, she must surely receive it. She provides as her entertainment a "swarthy traine" of gypsies, who live "At Natures charge," to dance the fifth antimasque. Since she, "Gorgon-like, turnes active men to stone" (l. 651), Mercury likewise banishes her.

Tyche / Fortune insists that she is deserving of heaven since she has served as deputy on earth of the departed Astraea, Goddess of Justice. She presents as the sixth antimasque a battle, "the modell of that martiall frame, / By which, when Crownes are stak'd, I rule the game" (ll. 715 - 16). Mercury dismisses her as "a deluding Phantome, / At best a blind guide, leading blinder fooles" (ll. 738 - 39).

Pleasure / Hedone is more difficult to dispatch, for she urges that honor and wealth are merely means to purchase her, that the wisest philosophers subscribe to her offices, that she is necessary to secure the propagation of mankind, and that she in fact is the general desire of all men. Her antimasque, the seventh of the play, consists of a dance by the five senses. Mercury ultimately condemns her as the "author of the first excesse / That drew this reformation (ll. 830 - 31).

By this time, Momus is so weary "of these tedious pleadings" (ll. 836 - 37) that he departs as abruptly as he came. Thus he is able to forestall the bands of suitors he sees rushing up.

Mercury outlines for the King and Queen the remaining action—a summoning of the spirits of their kingdoms and of the British heroes who will replace the exiled stars. The sphere vanishes and a new scene, of mountains, appears. A "more grave" antimasque (Number 8) of the "naturall Inhabitants of this Isle," Picts, Scots, and Irish, takes the form of a "Perica or Marshall [martial] dance."

Afterwards, a hill begins to rise, grows to a huge mountain, and covers the whole scene. In its middle portion are found seated the kingdoms of England, Scotland, and Ireland. Above them sits their Genius, with olive garland and cornucopia of "corne" and fruits. In the first song, Genius asks the kingdoms to call "your aged Priests, and chrystall streames" (l. 903) to warm the hearts of the royal pair, "Good and Faire" united. They oblige and a Chorus of Druids and rivers celebrates the light flowing from the King and Queen, who establish "Loves Hesperides" or fabled garden of the golden apples.

The "rock" (mountain) opens to emit from a cave masquers dressed like ancient British heroes, ushered forth by a troop of young lords and noblemen's sons, who dance first with their lights in their hands. Then the masquers descend into the room and dance their "entry."

During the second song, the kingdoms hear Genius praise the King and Queen once more and register their fear at the consequences of the removal of the royal twosome to Heaven. Genius reassures them:

> Jove shall not, to enrich the Skie,
> Beggar the Earth, their Fame shall flye
> From hence alone, and in the Spheare
> Kindle new Starres, whilst they rest here.
>   (ll. 992 - 95)

The kingdoms still are nonplussed, so Genius reminds them of the River Eridanus, "Above in streames of golden fire, / In silver waves below" (ll. 1000 - 1001). To their last doubt lest the triple union of England, Scotland, and Ireland crumble with his departure, Genius answers that he will renew his powers "In Concords pure immortall spring" and return with a "more active Vertue" (ll. 1006, 1008).

A "bright and transparent" cloud comes down from the farther part of the heavens and "embraceth the Genius, but so as through it all his body is seene." He and the cloud rise into the heavens and are seen no more. At the same time, the rock with the three kingdoms sinks and is hidden in the earth.

The masquers dance their main entertainment, and the scene shifts to a "delicious garden" with a palace in the distance. The Chorus addresses the Queen in the third song, honoring her "Halcyon beames" and offering a parade of British heroes. Expert in a different kind of "war," she can teach these heroes the art of true love. Afterwards, the Chorus retires, leaving the masquers to dance the revels ("which continued a great part of the night") with the ladies.

The King and Queen are seated once more, and a great cloud appears from one of the sides and stations itself in the middle of the scene. Two other clouds emerge from the farthest heavens—in one, Religion, Truth, and Wisdom; in the other, Concord, Government, and Reputation. The large cloud breaks open, emitting beams of light and revealing Eternity on a globe. In the firmament around him are fifteen stars, the stellified British heroes, among whom one stands out—"figuring" King Charles, with Windsor Castle seen afar off.

Eternity, Eusebia, Alethia, Sophia, Homonoia, Dicaearche, and Euphemia, in the fourth song, praise their respective virtues in Charles and Maria, wishing them timelessness, pure adoration, truth, wisdom, concord, rule, and "cleare" reputation. The King and Queen are then saluted for the aspirations that have brought them to the mountain's top beyond the "toyling Presse" and "panting Rout." They are to continue to guide men with their "influences" (a fitting pun), and these "Royall Turtles" [doves] must leave behind "ripe fruits" [children] so that "Scepters shall

bud, and Laurels blow / 'Bout their Immortall Throne" (ll. 1135 -
36).

The song having ended, the three clouds move from the scene,
leaving only a serene sky. The masquers introduce their last dance,
after whose conclusion the curtain falls.

II   *Occasion and Sources*

The motivation behind the writing of Carew's one masque is uncertain; but the quotation from the Latin poet Decius Magnus
Ausonius on the title page suggests that it is a command performance, "Caesar" being perhaps King Charles or, less likely, Inigo
Jones,[1] who designed and produced it. At any rate, *Coelum Britan-*
nicum was presented at Whitehall Palace on Shrove Tuesday,
February 18, 1633 / 34, with the King and the highest court
gentlemen taking parts. Its lavishness made it a fitting celebration
of the last night before Lent. The Master of the Revels, Sir Henry
Herbert, brother to the poets Sir Edward Herbert and George
Herbert, reported in his *Dramatic Records:* "On Shrovetusday
night . . . the Kinge dancte his Masque, accompanied with 11
lords, and attended with 10 pages. It was the noblest masque of my
time to this day [Herbert had held his position since 1623], the best
poetrye, best scenes, and the best habitts. The kinge and queene
were very well pleasd with my service, and the Q. was pleasd to tell
mee before the king, 'Pour les habits, elle n'avoit jamais rien vue de
si brave' [She had never seen anything so fine as the costumes]."[2] It
was probably the most daring and ambitious court masque, though
James Shirley's *Triumph of Peace*, a few months earlier at the Inns
of Court, is generally considered the most expensive masque of the
decade. It is also one of the longest court masques.

King Charles wanted *Coelum Britannicum* revived, but no record
of a second performance survives.[3] Nineteen of Inigo Jones's
designs are extant; and he may, as well, have at least helped with
the prose descriptions between episodes. The music was most likely
provided by Henry (perhaps by his brother William) Lawes. The
symbolism used for the gods is almost entirely traditional, following
the dictates of the very popular *Iconologia* (1611) of Cesar Ripa.
Much of the cost was lavished on the costumes, especially upon that
of King Charles. The whole production tends to call attention to the
waste of the Royalists, expending funds for such a project at a time
when the King was poor enough to be forced to haggle with Parlia-

ment and when few people outside the court found any credibility in the vision of a virtuous royal family, true "halcyons," perpetuating peace through an endless succession of similarly high-intentioned offspring. The paradox of the *forced* peace of the halcyon in Charles's reign somehow escaped the notice of both Carew, in whose poetry the image is frequently used, and the court.[4]

Carew's main indebtedness is to Giordano Bruno's *Spaccio de la Bestia Trionfante* (published in 1584 and dedicated to Sir Philip Sidney), a philosophical work based in turn on Lucian. It contains, in dialogue form, Carew's plot (Jupiter's or Jove's intention to reform heaven) and the figures of Momus and Mercury. In fact, Carew's only substantial changes are the introduction of topical allusions and the closing compliments to Charles and Maria. He occasionally condenses, as in ll. 356 - 70, where the vices of the skies are enumerated, or realigns the order in which materials are presented. Plutus is substituted for the Ricchezza of Bruno and Ripa; Hedone does not appear in Bruno; Fortune's part is much longer in Bruno, who also makes Eternity feminine. Nonetheless, Carew shows a certain wit in choosing his source. On Shrove / "Confession" Tuesday,[5] he is able to present an action in which the *gods confess* their sins, brought to this pass by the patterns of humanity—King Charles and Queen Henrietta Maria. Other sources are in evidence and suggest once more the varied influences at work in Carew. The pleading of their cases by the various gods and goddesses, for example, may recall Donne's *Ignatius His Conclave.*

The vision of "Loves Hesperides" at the end of the masque salutes the supposedly Platonic "court of love" established by the Queen and mingles the styles, according to one critic,[6] of Tasso, Donne, and Jonson. Contrastingly, Hazlitt finds the style of its "familiar dramatic dialogue approaching writers of Queen Anne's reign rather than Queen Elizabeth's."[7] Schoff is equally convinced that its aura is Elizabethan, particularly the speeches of Momus: "This fountain of satirical nonsense has Elizabethan gaiety rather than the harshness of Jonson, Donne, or Marston; and so do most of Momus's other lines. Thus one feels again that Carew derives from that older, yet more youthful tradition: this time in terms of Sim Eyre [of Thomas Dekker's *The Shoemakers' Holiday*] and [Shakespeare's] Falstaff."[8] He also recognizes the specific influence of François Rabelais on Momus, who is allowed to list Rabelais and Pietro Aretine (the latter also referred to in "A Rapture") as

"Bird[s] of mine owne feather," while repudiating the "meere counterfeit," "arrant Mountebanke," Guez de Balzac.[9].

Carew's masque is, of course, indebted to the masques of Jonson and to Jonson's development of the antimasque (Carew's has eight antimasques!), especially to his *Pleasure Reconciled to Virtue*.[10] It likewise shows the influence of the mechanical contrivances of the Continental masques, as well as of the ingenuity of Jones, in its use of a cloud machine and a mechanized mountain. Nevertheless, its improvements and achievements were well received. The Description of the Scene (154) records this response to the "ornament": ". . . for the Invention and various composition, was the newest and most gracious that hath beene done in this place." And when the mountain with the three kingdoms sinks into the earth: "This strange spectacle gave great cause of admiration, but especially how so huge a machine, and of that great height could come from under the Stage, which was but six foot high" (179).

III   Unity

Carew has contributed to the basic materials of Bruno's dialogue the encircling theme of the glory of Britain and of her present rulers. The amalgam has been accomplished amazingly well. The two female figures on the vases of the ornament sound the patriotic note of the masque with their symbolization of the "glory of Princes" and of mansuetude, the former individualized by the impresses of Charles and Maria and stressed throughout the play. Mercury's first speech not only foreshadows in its reference to the "three warlike Nations" the mountain of the three kingdoms upcoming, but enlists the attribute of mildness associated with the current reign and the peacefulness of the 1630s. Characteristically, "doctrine" early in the masque is dressed out symbolically in the crescendo of mechanical contrivances at the end. The two smaller clouds thus represent Religion, Truth, and Wisdom; and Government, Reputation, and Concord, respectively. The enduring influence of Charles and Maria is stressed in their exemplary lives imitated throughout their own court, the world, and heaven, where the gods have looked into the crystal mirror (once more in Carew!) of their reign, and in the fact that the "lower globe" will owe its light to these "British stars," as is borne out at the end of the masque. The ideas of Mercury are reiterated in a very different key by the prose of Momus. Again, Mercury, in his bridging speech following the seventh antimasque and Momus's departure, restates the same views as he tells of their upcoming portrayal (ll. 848 - 70).

The antimasque that follows, of the "naturall Inhabitants of this Isle," Picts, Scots, and Irish, activates the patriotic notes of Mercury's speech and has likewise been carefully provided for. The masque presents in minature the whole history of Britain, which has culminated, at least in the chauvinism of Carew's treatment, in the advent of CARLOMARIA, in the merging of Britain and heaven. The opening scene, accordingly, has resembled "the ruines of some great City of the ancient Romans, or civiliz'd Brittaines." The "ancient worthies of the British Isles" take their rightful places in the eighth sphere, once the expulsion of the stars is completed. The Druids of Britain and its streams (similar to the water images of another "British" masque, Milton's *Comus*, with its treatment of Sabrina) help the three kingdoms and their Genius celebrate the King and Queen. After the dance of the "ancient inhabitants" (Antimasque 8), from the cave in the mountain come the ancient heroes themselves, preceded by the young lords and noblemen's sons in a reemphasis of the continuity of Britain's history. In the third song, the Chorus begs the Queen to refurbish those heroes, who excelled in acts of war and courage, in the robes of peace. Arthur and St. George, for example, must have "Plant[ed] in their Martiall hands, Warr's seat, / Your peacefull pledges of warme snow" (ll. 1036 - 37).

Clearly, Carew has an obstacle to overcome here. He has to celebrate both Britian and her present rulers, showing the great strides of the present without diminishing those of the past. He accomplishes this feat by dwelling on the necessity of the warrior-heroes of the past, whose stellifying is made possible by the deeds of Charles and Maria. He has a similar problem dealing with the future. He cannot entirely shut off the possibility of the greatness of succeeding sovereigns, yet he has Eternity extravagantly call for Time to stand still "Since Good is here so perfect, as no Worth / Is left for After-Ages to bring forth" (ll. 1095 - 96). It is perhaps the greatest of ironies that this cessation is effectively what happened, from the viewpoint of the royal prerogative at least, halted by the 1649 regicide of Charles I, until 1660 and the restoration of Charles II. The historical dangers latent in this masque burst forth when the *French* Queen becomes the instrument, with her "court of love," by which the British heroes are made palatable for the present reign of peace and for Britain's new colony, the eighth sphere. Again, the insurmountable, fantastic problems of this Royalist dream are suggested in the fanciful and outmoded Ptolemaic materials upon which it depends. In fact, the return to the Ptolemaic universe demarks, for later audiences at least, the retroversion of the whole Caroline court.

IV *Contrast and Humor*

Carew was too much of a skeptic to remain on this ethereal level at every moment. As masque and antimasque are manipulated in the course of the plot, so too are the two "presenters," Mercury and Momus (the latter being garbed to symbolize Ripa's Discordia), who offer contrasting views of the play's fiber. Mercury, in verse, constantly assumes the high style; Momus, in prose, the low. From his opening greeting, "Goodden Cozen *Hermes*," the audience instinctively grasps that he is more the London "cit.'' or citizen than the denizen of heaven. Exaggeration is his method, for he knows full well that his is Mercury's "nine thousandth nine hundred ninety ninth Legation." His mock-epic presentment of credentials is one of the best pieces of the masque: "My name is *Momus-ap-Somnus-ap-Erebus-ap-Chaos-ap-Demogorgon-ap-Eternity*. My Offices and Titles are, The Supreme Theomastix, Hupercrittique of manners, Protonotarie of abuses, Arch-Informer, Dilator Generall, Universall Calumniator, Eternall Plaintiffe, and perpetuall Foreman of the Grand Inquest. My privileges are an ubiquitary, circumambulatory, speculatory, interrogatory, redargutory immunity over all the privy lodgings, behind hangings, dores, curtaines, through keyholes, chinkes, windowes, about all Veneriall lobbies, Skonces or Redoubts . . ." (ll. 134 - 43). To hear him talk, half of heaven's mischiefs are his doing; e. g., "as when Saturne guelt [castrated] his father."

Momus may be thought of as the alter ego of Eternity, who figures in the ending of the masque. The two provide another of the techniques of contrast implicit in the genre of masque. Structurally, Momus drops out just prior to Mercury's announcement that "The sacred hand of bright Eternitie [will] / Mould you to Stars, and fix you in the Spheare" (ll. 863 - 64). Carew suggests that Momus is "purified" in Eternity, as antimasque is replaced by the unified vision of the masque proper. Further, Carew may be offering through Momus-Eternity the opinion that the Comic Spirit is necessary to both the "antic" and the ethereal worlds—to all dispensations and reigns.

Before his departure, then, Momus carries the play's humor. Where Mercury tells of Jove's determined Reformation as the result of the "great Example" of the King and Queen, Momus believes that the godhead has taken such a step "out of the consideration of the decay of his natural abilities" (ll. 197 - 98).[11] And the juxtaposition of the termagant Juno with *breviary*, not to mention its length and the subsequent pun on the term, is a testimony to how "seriously" Momus takes the whole venture: Jove has "taken his oath on *Junos* Breviary, religiously kissing the two-leav'd booke, never to stretch his limbs more betwixt adulterous sheets . . ." (ll. 202 - 204).

Momus knows his proverbs so well that he understands when they must have a change. After the third antimasque, a dance by various vices, he quips: "From henceforth it shall be no more said in the Proverbe, when you would expresse a riotous Assembly, That hell, but heaven is broke loose . . ." (ll. 376 - 78). The versatility of his rhetoric and his consciousness of his rhetorical powers are shown as well when, upon concluding his discourse on "the politique state of heaven to this trimme Audience," he asks: "Am not I in election to be a tall Statesman thinke you, that can repeat a passage at a Counsell-table thus punctually?" (ll. 222 - 24). Again, he takes it upon himself to provide a mock - Proclamation of Reformation "Given at Our Palace in *Olympus* the first day of the first month, in the first yeare of the Reformation" (ll. 424 - 65). He likewise parodies the legal jargon of Carew's Inns of Court experience as he would censure Tyche or Fortune *pro falso clamore* were it not for her being blind.

The humorous satire of the masque, much of it topical additions by Carew, is purveyed by Momus, though the following report of reformations, while it is akin to English reforms of the period,[12] comes primarily from Bruno:

Injunctions are gone out to the Nectar Brewers, for the purging of the heavenly Beverage of a narcotique weed [tobacco] which hath rendred the Idaeaes confus'd in the Divine intellects. . . . *Baccus* hath commanded all Tavernes to be shut, and no liquor drawne after tenne at night. *Cupid* must goe no more so scandalously naked, but is enjoyned to make him breeches though of his mothers petticoates. *Ganimede* is forbidden the Bedchamber, and must onely minister in publique. The gods must keep no Pages, nor Groomes of their Chamber under the age of 25. and those provided of a competent stocke of beard.

(ll. 237 - 53)

The reader is left to wonder whether there is not something of the *roman à clef*, of topical satire, about Carew's choices of tales of the gods.

Momus is Carew's vehicle for laughing genially at his own "profession," as Momus rails at the poets, "who enjoy by Patent a particular privilege to draw downe any of the Deities from Twelf-night till Shrove-tuesday . . . [but who] have as yet never invited me to these Solemnities . . ." (ll. 127 - 31). In Momus's mock-proclamation, the constellations are cashiered and an "Inquisition erected to expunge in the Ancient, and suppresse in the moderne and succeeding Poems and Pamphlets, all past, present, and future mention of these abjur'd heresies . . ." (ll. 217 - 20). Moreover, it is these "Libertines of Antiquity, the Ribald Poets" (ll. 207 - 208), who have immortalized these "strumpets" in the stars in the first place. After the first antimasque, of natural deformity, Momus casts a satirical eye at the analogies poured out by the poets upon their ladies: "Doe not you faire Ladies acknowledge your selves deeply engaged now to those Poets your servants, that in the height of commendation have rais'd your beauties to a parallell with such ex-act proportions, or at least rank'd you in their spruce society?" (ll. 308 - 13). And Poverty's "perpetuall conversation with Poets and Philosophers," he is certain, should have armed her with better logic (ll. 628 - 30). Expanding his target area somewhat, Momus reacts to Mercury's denunciation of the zodiacal sign of the crab: "This Crab, I confesse, did ill become the heavens; but there is another that more infests the Earth, and makes such a solstice in the politer Arts and Sciences, as they have not beene observed for many Ages to have made any sensible advance . . ." (ll. 347 - 51).

The other topical allusions are usually also satirical and humorous, as in the case of disposing of the deposed constellations by dumping them in New England. But they may record simply everyday events and personages, as in the reference to the astrologers John Booker and Richard Allestree (ll. 405 - 406), the analogy between the Star-Chamber of Westminster and the eighth sphere of fixed stars (though the political overtones of that apart-ment make the allusion satirical now), and the reference to the tapestries in the House of Lords (ll. 430 - 32). Certainly, the allusion in this passage is to the infamous Gunpowder Plot of November 5, 1605: "*Vulcan* was brought to an Oretenus [a legal proceeding] and fined, for driving in a plate of Iron into one of the Sunnes Chariot-wheeles and frost-nailing his horses upon the fifth of *November* last, for breach of a penall Statute prohibiting worke upon Holydayes . . ." (ll. 255 - 59). Some allusions are, of course, more obscure now, as Momus's plea for using certain of the banished constellations (ll. 410 - 13).

V *The Poetry*

Several critics have expressed surprise at the sustained poetic power of the blank verse of *Coelum Britannicum*. Schoff, for example, speaks of the "long-breathed, muscular lines"[13] exemplified by Mercury's account of the zodiac (ll. 327 - 38). Mercury's speeches are generally first-rate and show an effective use of catalectic lines (as 645 and 649 below) and occasional elision (l. 661 below), as in this simultaneous rebuke of Poverty and declaration of true heroism:

> Thou dost presume too much, poore needy wretch,
> To claime a station in the Firmament,
> Because thy humble Cottage, or thy Tub
> Nurses some lazie or Pedantique virtue   645
> In the cheape Sun-shine, or by shady springs
> With roots and pot-hearbs; where thy rigid hand,
> Tearing those humane passions from the mind,
> Upon whose stockes faire blooming vertues flourish,   649
> Degradeth Nature, and benummeth sense,
> And Gorgon-like, turnes active men to stone.
> We not require the dull society
> Of your necessitated Temperance,
> Of that unnaturall stupidity
> That knowes nor joy nor sorrow; nor your forc'd
> Falsly exalted passive Fortitude
> Above the active: This low abject brood,
> That fix their seats in mediocrity,
> Become your servile minds; but we advance
> Such vertues onely as admit excesse,
> Brave bounteous Acts, Regall Magnificence,   661
> All-seeing Prudence, Magnanimity
> That knowes no bound, and that Heroicke vertue
> For which Antiquity hath left no name,
> But patternes onely, such as *Hercules*,
> *Achilles, Theseus*. Backe, to thy loath'd cell,
> And when thou seest the new enlightned Spheare,
> Study to know but what those Worthies were.
>   (ll. 642 - 68)

In the blank verse, Carew has achieved the close, analytical voice that was successful only occasionally in the poems. His repudiation of Hedone (ll. 809 - 35), like the above a pastiche of traditional images, also acquires an effectiveness of the whole largely by the argumentative power of the unrhymed iambic pentameter lines.[14]

Carew is also capable of endowing his false speakers with telling persuasiveness. Fortune's claims are derivative, but, especially as she moves to the last lines, poignant:

> For since *Astraea* fled to heaven, I sit
> Her Deputy on Earth, I hold her skales
> And weigh mens Fates out, who have made me blind,
> Because themselves want eyes to see my causes,
> Call me inconstant, 'cause my workes surpasse
> The shallow fathom of their human reason;
> Yet here, like blinded Justice, I dispence
> With my impartiall hands, their constant lots
> And if desertlesse, impious men engrosse
> My best rewards, the fault is yours, you gods,
> That scant your graces to mortalitie,
> And niggards of your good, scarce spare the world
> One vertuous, for a thousand wicked men.
> It is no error to conferre dignity,
> But to bestow it on a vicious man;
> I gave the dignity, but you made the vice,
> Make you men good, and I'le make good men happy.
>   (ll. 687 - 703)

Pleasure, too, has some truth in her plaintive self-justifications:

> Beyond me nothing is, I am the Gole,
> The journeyes end, to which the sweating world,
> And wearied Nature travels . . . .
>   (ll. 772 - 74)

Milton also wrote great poetry for Comus (whose masque was forthcoming within a few months), but he had the Lady to pitch the opposite view in golden notes.[15]

There remains an air of disengagement about Mercury's speeches; they are somewhat cold, perhaps because the defendant has no opportunity for the give-and-take of debate. Also, there lingers about Mercury the taint of perfunctoriness, and one remembers that Momus has in his opening speech taunted the less-than-noble descent of the Messenger of the Gods. But, then, except in rare instances, there remains an air of disengagement about Mercury's master, Thomas Carew.

The best parts of the masque are those comic moments of Momus's posturing, parts that make one wish that the kind of poetry Carew felt obliged to write in his particular period had allowed more scope for humor. Also fine are the closely argued speeches where all that he had learned from Donne could be brought into play.

The modern response to *Coelum Britannicum* must be colored by subsequent historical events. One never quite forgets, however gorgeous it is and however much one would want the grandiose sentiments to be true, the following contemporary response to the extravagance of this and all court masques: "Oh that they would once give over these Things, or lay them aside for a Time, and bend all their Endeavours to make the King Rich! For it gives me no Satisfaction, who am but a looker on, to see a rich Commonwealth, a rich People, and the Crown poor. God direct them to remedy this quickly."[16]

CHAPTER 7

Carew's Reputation and Importance

I *Reputation*

WITH only ten poems (some anonymous, some probably un-
authorized) and *Coelum Britannicum* published while he was
living, Carew would not be expected to have a wide contemporary
reputation. Like the works of his peers, however, his circulated in
manuscript, were popular, and gained him the label of another
court libertine. By 1640 (the year of the publication of the first edition of his poems), Sir Edward Dering, while delivering before the
House of Commons Richard Robson's "Kent Petition against
Episcopacy," denounced the outbreak of "lascivious," "idle," and
"unprofitable" works, including Carew's *Poems*.[1] The anonymous
satire, *The Great Assises Holden in Parnassus by Apollo and his
assessours* (1645), probably by the Puritan poet George Wither,
features Carew and other poets being considered for jury duty at an
inquest into pornography. Along with his friends Thomas May and
William Davenant, Carew is deemed a "renowned poet" and "man
of worth" ("If wit may passe for worth"). Nonetheless, the prisoner
refuses to have him a member of the jury. "Learn'd Scaliger"
attempts to defend Carew, finally giving the poet himself the floor.
A "palinode" or recantation ensues, with the implication that "A
Rapture" is primarily responsible for his damaged reputation.[2]

In a manuscript note, William Oldys summarizes Carew's contemporary reputation as a poet in this way: "His Sonnets were more
in request than any poet's of his time, that is between 1630 &
1640."[3] His close friends paid him equally high tribute, for even
this "condemnation" by Sir John Suckling in "A Sessions of the
Poets" (1638)—"His Muse was hard bound, and th' issue of's
brain / Was seldom brought forth but with trouble and pain"—is
playful; and its sting is tempered by the enduring close relations
between the two poets. Though, as has been shown in Chapter 4,

Carew was known as one of the "Sons of Ben," he was his "own man." The Earl of Clarendon in his autobiography pictures him from about 1625 - 32 as one of his circle and speaks of Carew's poetry as at least the equal of, and perhaps as surpassing, that of anyone else at the time. His wit is complimented, for example, by Thomas Randolph, Aurelian Townshend,[4] Lord Herbert of Cherbury, and William Davenant; his "language" in the love poetry, by James Shirley, William Cartwright, Robert Baron, and John Leigh. Others, including Randolph, mention specifically his "Celia" and thus reaffirm his popularity as an amorous poet.

Individual poems exerted their own influences. As might be expected, "A Rapture" made an impression on several poets, among them John Cleveland, Randolph, Cartwright, and Richard Crashaw, and perhaps also on the anonymous author of *The Tragedy of Nero* (1624). Henry Jacob translated "Ingratefull beauty threatned" into Latin elegiacs, and the elegy on Donne apparently affected other commemorations of that poet's death in the 1633 memorial volume and later influenced Robert Blair.[5] Though specific influence is not confirmed, many contemporary and later poets (e.g., William Drummond of Hawthornden, Thomas Bateson, Sidney Godolphin, and Robert Heath), in addition to those already cited, offer parallels to Carew's works. Probably the most influential single poem is "Aske me no more where Jove bestowes," of which several versions exist. There are seventeenth-century adaptations and parodies of it, including a political treatment. Pope used it in the *Dunciad* and Tennyson in *The Princess*. Pope also used lines from "Obsequies to the Lady Anne Hay," and Dryden adapted the last couplet of "A cruell Mistris." Lucy Ashton's song in Sir Walter Scott's *The Bride of Lammermoor* echoes both "Good counsel to a young Maid" (13) and "Conquest by flight."[6]

Toward the end of the seventeenth century, Carew's reputation weakened. The first four editions of his poetry were printed in 1640, 1642, 1651, and 1670. The next did not appear until Thomas Davies, using the 1670 edition, produced a new volume in 1772, with reprints by others coming out in 1793 and 1810.[7] Many musical settings of his poems appeared in print during the century, and his poems themselves are frequently preserved in the miscellanies of the day.[8]

As Carew's memory receded in time, the assessments not only became more general, but more dependent, with little reading of the poems themselves. Acclaiming Carew's delicate wit and poetic fancy, Edward Phillips, in *Theatrum Poetarum Anglicanorum* (1675), set the stage for William Winstanley, Anthony à Wood, and others. In praising Edmund Waller as not inferior to Carew, he also suggested comparisons that have prevailed into the modern period, as critics speak of Carew anticipating the line of development through Waller and into Pope and the Augustans.

Pope himself called Carew "A bad Waller" and found him Waller's model in "matter," but not in versification. He included Carew in the "school of Waller," but perhaps damned him most in the *Epistle to Augustus*, whose tag of the "mob of gentlemen who wrote with ease" has endured. Nevertheless, as was shown above, Pope drew on Carew in his own works; and Joseph Warton mentions Carew as among the "dregs" from whom Pope "collected gold." Here is Arthur H. Nethercot's summation of Carew during the "Age of Pope": "Carew's lightness and grace preserved him a minor place in the estimation of a few of the 'curious,' but even then strong objections were often made to his extravagancies [along with those of others classed as Metaphysical]. He also maintained a slight reputation as a courtier and as the writer of a masque."[9]

If his own age praised his smoothness, the eighteenth century seemed to prefer Waller's smoothness; and, as has been suggested, only recently has the continuity from Carew to Pope been stressed. He continued to be touched on in the eighteenth century—for example, by Theophilus Cibber, the second edition of the *Biographia Britannica* (1778 - 93), David Baker, Reverend James Granger, Thomas Percy, Joseph Cockfield (who speaks of him in 1766 as "almost forgotten"), Joseph Warton's 1797 edition of Pope, Thomas Warton, Joseph Ritson, George Ellis, and Robert Anderson (who took exception to Johnson's omission of Carew).[10] One of the most interesting of these generally derivative sketches is John Nichols's in a *Select Collection of Poems* (1780 - 82): Donne is alluded to only as being among "the first men of the age" to admire Carew.[11] Henry Headley, in *Select Beauties of Ancient English Poetry*, uses Phillips, the *Biographia Britannica*, Percy, and others but adds a distinctive contribution in assessing Carew and Waller: "Waller is too exclusively considered as the first man who brought versification to any thing [*sic*] like its present standard. Carew's pretensions to the same merit are seldom sufficiently either considered or allowed."[12]

By 1820, Carew is set forth by William Hazlitt in his *Lectures on the Age of Elizabeth* as an "elegant court-trifler" who uses "far-fetched and improbable conceits."[13] This notion tended to hold

through W. J. Courthope's *A History of English Poetry* (1924), but
at least sincere appraisal of the poetry itself was undertaken in this
last. Moreover, in the interim between Hazlitt and Courthope, such
a resolute individual as Henry David Thoreau could single out 11.
642 - 68 of *Coelum Britannicum*, Mercury's condemnation of "The
Pretensions of Poverty," as Thoreau labels them, for inclusion in
Walden. Modern criticism for some time went along with Hazlitt's
presumption of Carew's inconsequence, though Joseph Ebsworth's
earlier saccharinity (1893) should not be overlooked. Arthur Vincent
(1899) and R. G. Howarth (1931) yield sound criticism.

Carew regained some stature with the modern recovery of the
Metaphysicals. Since his inclusion in Sir Herbert J. C. Grierson's
*Metaphysical Lyrics and Poems of the Seventeenth Century. Donne
to Butler* (1921), interest in Carew has generally focused on his classification. In his several books on the Metaphysicals, George
Williamson has helped to establish Carew as a disciple of Donne,
though on the "fringe" of the Donne tradition. Contrastingly, F. R.
Leavis (1936) found a "line of wit" from Jonson (and Donne)
through Carew and Marvell to Pope. Rhodes Dunlap's standard edition came in 1949, its introduction and notes stressing mingled influences on Carew, including Giambattista Marino and the
Baroque. More recently, Rufus Blanshard, as has been shown, has
linked Carew with Jonson, with the other Cavaliers, and with
Renaissance rhetoricians, notably George Puttenham. Another
realignment has taken shape in Francis Schoff's claim that Carew is
a "Son of Spenser."

Still, there has been until now only one book devoted to Carew.
Edward I. Selig, in *The Flourishing Wreath*, has examined Carew's
vers de société, song lyrics, imagery, derivativeness, five poems
representing the "heart of [Carew's] lyrical achievement"[14] ("Good
counsel to a young Maid," "The Spring," "Boldnesse in love," "To
A. L. Perswasions to love," and "A Song"—"Aske me no more
where Jove bestowes"), and his verse-epistles. Selig has been especially helpful in his study of the relationship between music and
Carew's poetry. His book concludes that "Carew's art is perfect *of
its kind*."[15]

II *Place and Importance*

Carew's importance as a poet who reflects and synthesizes the
currents of seventeenth-century poetry is firmly established. One

can get some glimpse in him of about every turn the poetry of that period was taking. One does not find all these turns as a practical matter in Donne and Jonson. And were it not for the fact that they are such outstanding poets with "schools" of followers, he might already have received more attention. As it is, there is little likelihood that modern critics or modern readers will stop saying, "This is not Donne, but it is good."

Carew is almost always enjoyable to read and is only infrequently obscure. In spite of the limitations of the genres within which he worked (amorous lyric, elegy, occasional poem, masque), he has a remarkable variety—in treatment of subject and in techniques of versification. Whether addressing Celia, his "mistress," or some more obscure female, he can show all conceivable portraits and moods of the lover and of love. He moves surprisingly and lithely from adulation and rebuke to an empathy with the woman's point of view, to cynical enjoyment, to ethereal idealism, or to wry advice for other lovers. Hyperbole is his chief weapon in these ventures; but he brings to Ovidian metamorphosis, Classical allusions, "unnatural natural history," and the engulfment of Petrarchan gems and caskets, nests, phoenix, gums and spices, halcyon, pearls, eddies, and "blubbered eyes" (which seem to be his favorite borrowings) a directness and force of his own.

Most often, his directness and force result from concentration on developing closely an image or idea within the poem and from his perhaps salient trait, the effective final couplet. These qualities derive as well from his customary tone, both conversational and peremptory. He manages to create the feeling—no small matter when one works within established molds—that his concerns are above all urgent, or, in his sweetest lyrics (the poems frequently as perfect as the gems with which he fills them) that they are timeless. For the timeless quality, his silver verses, especially in the dominant tetrameter and pentameter couplets, can take some credit; they are so close to music that Henry Lawes often found his task partially done by the poet. More surprising are Carew's serious interest in the tasks of poetry and his critical bent. He still has not been excelled in his appreciation of Donne.

Some may object that he is in the court but not of it, that he commits himself to none of the pressing political or religious issues of the day. It is a grievous fault but a fault of the first Caroline court in general and one which it grievously answered. Carew made poetry walk in step with the everyday occurrences of the nobility of the time. One could just as easily object that Milton did not present the court at all, and yet Milton's poetry is in some ways more aristocratic.

The major and the minor poets bring balance to the portrait of an age. The virtual sacrilege of *Coelum Britannicum* is a foil for *Paradise Lost,* as the masque itself is a foil for *Comus.* It unconsciously sums up an era as Carew's "darke riddles of the amorous art" ("A Lady rescued from death by a Knight . . . ," l. 10) and "mutuall change / Of soules" ("An Hymeneall Dialogue," ll. 13 - 14) sum up at least two centuries of love and love poetry. Even if it were true that "Carew is so typical that he has almost no qualities of his own," [16] he would deserve attention for that reason alone.

It is true that he was sometimes discomfited by the role of court poet he chose to play. He can perform extraordinarly well in witty, erotic poems or in golden love poems, but he seems to feel most comfortable in the poems where he allows himself to indulge in lengthy, logical analysis after the fashion of Donne. Often when he attempts to intellectualize in his poems, however, he loses the sense of structured argument at which he can excel, or he loses sight of the woman with whom he is supposed to be in dialogue. Only in the elegy on Donne and in occasional sections of individual love poems did he match Donne's prowess in the close style. Perhaps this is why Carew chose to stay most often in the restricted limits of the court poet of the day. More amazing is his grasp of those limits and of the various approaches to poetry available in his time.

Notes and References

Chronology

1. The first date is reckoned according to the Julian or Old Style Calendar. The second is the civil or fiscal year beginning on March 25. This Gregorian or New Style Calendar was adopted in England in 1752.

Chapter One

1. Arthur Vincent, ed., *Poems of Thomas Carew* (London, 1899), p. xix.

2. *The Poems of Thomas Carew with His Masque Coelum Britannicum* (Oxford, 1949), p. xiv. The link between the name and a plow persists, appearing, for example, in William Styron's *The Confessions of Nat Turner* (New York, 1966), p. 125.

3. See Jack Dalglish, ed., *Eight Metaphysical Poets* (London, 1961), p. 147; Vincent, p. xxviii. Sir Arthur Quiller-Couch, *Adventures in Criticism* (Cambridge, 1926), p. 14, points out that Carew's editor, Ebsworth, in his dedicatory prelude, is mistaken in pronouncing the name "Carew;" he also scans verses from seventeenth-century poems to show that the pronunciation is "Carey." Cf. Dunlap, p. xiv, n.

4. So Sir Matthew describes his son's revelation of his purposes. The letter quoted in the text was written to Carleton on October 4, 1617. See Dunlap, pp. xxii - xxviii, for this and Matthew Carew's other letters to Sir Dudley.

5. Dunlap gives Carew's three letters in Appendix C, pp. 201 - 206. This compliment occurs in the one dated September 2, 1616.

6. In "Upon T. C. having the P.," given in Dunlap, p. 209, Sir John Suckling twits Carew for suffering from the "French disease."

7. Both offices were largely ceremonial by Carew's day. Members of the Privy Chamber attended the King in his private quarters. The Sewer in Ordinary originally helped with the arrangements of the royal table.

8. Both are given in Dunlap, pp. 211 - 12.

9. *Epistolae Ho-Elianae*. Cited in Vincent, pp. xxiv - xxv.

10. *The Life of Edward Earl of Clarendon . . . Written by Himself.* Cited in Dunlap, p. xxxix.

11. George Sandys (1578 - 1644) was also a Gentleman of the Privy Chamber. He is best known for his translation of the Psalms and of Ovid's *Metamorphoses*.

12. Dunlap, pp. 93 - 94. All references for the works of Carew are to this edition, and page numbers are given in the text in parentheses.

13. Pp. xliv - xlv, 244 - 45.

14. According to a letter to the writer from the Lord Chamberlain's Office, St. James's Palace, dated October 1, 1974.

15. Among the poems offering suggestions of Donne's influence are "Secresie protested" (11), "To my Mistresse in absence" (22), "Eternitie of love protested" (23 - 24), "To T. H. a Lady resembling my Mistress" (26 - 27), "Upon a Ribband" (29), "Upon the sickness of E. S." (31 - 32), "To one that desired to know my Mistris" (39 - 40), "A Rapture" (49 - 53), "Maria Wentworth" (56), "Incommunicabilitie of Love" (62), the elegy on Donne (71 - 74), "To my friend G. N. from Wrest" (86 - 89), "The Comparison" (98 - 99), "The tinder" (104), "The tooth-ach cured by a kisse" (109 - 10), "Upon a Mole in Celias bosome" (113 - 14), "To *Celia*, upon Love's Ubiquity" (123 - 24), "An Excuse of absence" (131), "On the Duke of Buckingham" (57), "An Hymeneall Dialogue" (66), "Obsequies to the Lady Anne Hay" (67 - 68), "Loves Courtship" (107 - 108), and "An Hymeneall Song on the Nuptials of the Lady *Ann Wentworth*, and the Lord *Lovelace*" (114 - 15). Carew shows Donne's fondness for alchemical images and calentures. See also Chapter 4. (In this and the following footnotes on Carew's sources, the writer acknowledges help from Dunlap and other critics.)

16. Jonson's influence is shown less in individual poems, but see especially "To the Reader of Master William Davenant's Play" (97), "To Ben. Johnson" (64 - 65), "To Saxham" (27 - 29), "To my friend G. N. from Wrest" (86 - 89), "Mediocritie in love rejected" (12 - 13), "To my worthy Friend, M. D'avenant, Upon his Excellent Play, *The Just Italian*" (95 - 96), and "To the King at his entrance into Saxham" (30 - 31). All of the elegies and country-house poems and Carew's masque should be compared to Jonson's efforts in those genres. See Chapters 4 - 6.

17. For Ovid, see, for example, "A flye that flew into my Mistris her eye" (37 - 38), "Celia singing" (38), "Truce in Love entreated" (41), "A Rapture" (49 - 53), "Incommunicabilitie of Love" (62), "Upon Master W. Mountague his returne from travell" (77 - 78), "Upon my Lord Chiefe Justice" (83 - 84), and "To my friend G. N. from Wrest" (87 - 89); for Catullus, see "Secresie protested" (11), "A Rapture" (49 - 53), "A New-yeares gift. To the King" (89 - 90), "To his mistresse retiring in affection" (129 - 30), "To my inconstant Mistris" (15 - 16), "To her in absence. A Ship" (23), and "Good Counsell to a young Maid" (25); for Propertius, see "To my inconstant Mistris" (15 - 16), "Ingratefull beauty threatned" (17 - 18), "The willing Prisoner to his Mistris" (37), "On the Marriage of T. K. and C.C. the morning stormie" (79 - 80), and "The Complement" (99 - 101). Minor Latin influences are Lucretius and Horace (especially in the Jonsonian poems).

18. For the probable influence of Francesco Petrarch himself, see "The Spring" (3), "My mistris commanding me to returne her letters" (9 - 11), "A prayer to the Wind" (11 - 12), "Mediocritie in love rejected" (12 - 13),

"A flye that flew into my Mistris her eye" (37 - 38), "Truce in Love entreated" (41), and "A Rapture" (49 - 53). A good discussion of the Petrarchan tradition as it is applicable to Carew is to be found in Francis G. Schoff, "Thomas Carew: Son of Ben or Son of Spenser?" *Discourse*, 1 (1958), 8 - 24.

19. Primarily, the French poets of the Pléiade, who had influenced such sixteenth-century English poets as Edmund Spenser and Samuel Daniel. For probable influence of Pierre de Ronsard, see "Perswasions to enjoy" (16), "The Spring" (3), and the epitaph on Mary Villiers ("This little Vault . . . ," 54); for Desportes, see "My mistris commanding me to returne her letters" (9 - 11), "Truce in Love entreated" (41), and "To the Painter" (106 - 107); for Pontus de Tyard, see "The willing Prisoner to his Mistris" (37).

20. For Tasso, see "A cruell Mistris" (8), "Mediocritie in love rejected" (12 - 13), "In the person of a Lady to her inconstant servant" (40), "A Rapture" (49 - 53), and "Upon a Mole in Celias bosome" (113 - 14); for Guarini, see "A flye that flew into my Mistris her eye" (37 - 38), "Upon a Mole in Celias bosome" (113 - 14), "A Ladies prayer to Cupid" (131), and "An Excuse of absence" (131); for Marino, see "To A. L. Perswasions to love" (4 - 6), "A beautifull Mistris" (7), "Lips and Eyes" (6), "A Looking-Glasse" (19), "Upon the sicknesse of (E. S.)" (31 - 32), "Red, and white Roses" (46 - 47), "For a Picture where a Queen Laments over the Tombe of a slaine Knight" (81), "The Complement" (99 - 101), and "The tinder" (104).

21. For Carew's revisions of his poems, see Dunlap, pp. lvii - lix.

22. Cf. John Erskine, *The Elizabethan Lyric, A Study* (New York, 1903), pp. 233 - 34, who traces Carew's standard form to Thomas Campion.

23. Carew's "Neo-Platonism" may be only generalized borrowings. For ideas suggesting comparison with the doctrines of Giovanni Pico Della Mirandola, however, see these poems: "A divine Mistris" (6 - 7), "Ingratefull beauty threatned" (17 - 18), "Celia singing" (39), "Epitaph on the Lady S." (55), "To A. D. unreasonable distrustfull of her owne beauty" (84 - 86), and "An Hymeneall Song on the Nuptials of the Lady *Ann Wentworth*, and the Lord *Lovelace*" (114 - 15).

24. See Alan J. Biggs, "Carew and Shakespeare," *N&Q*, N.S., 3 (1956), 225.

25. The verse has been studied by Charles J. Sembower, "A Note on the Verse Structure of Carew," *Studies in Language and Literature in Celebration of the Seventieth Birthday of James Morgan Hart* (New York, 1910), pp. 456 - 66, and Rufus A. Blanshard, "Thomas Carew's Master Figures," *Boston University Studies in English*, 3 (1957), 214 - 27.

Chapter Two

1. P. xx.
2. P. xxx.

3. The legal language is conventional.

4. Sembower uses this poem to show Carew, "at his best," merging form and meaning.

5. See Edward I. Selig, *The Flourishing Wreath: A Study of Thomas Carew's Poetry* (New Haven, 1958), pp. 105 - 106.

6. See Earl Miner, *The Cavalier Mode from Jonson to Cotton* (Princeton, 1971), p. 106. Another interesting view of the poem is to be found in H. M. Richmond, *The School of Love: The Evolution of the Stuart Love Lyric* (Princeton, 1964), pp. 70 - 71.

7. The opposition between body and mind occurs with some frequency in Carew's verse; e.g., "Disdaine returned" (18), "A Looking-Glasse" (19), "To my Mistresse in absence" (22), "Eternitie of love protested" (23 - 24), "Upon a Ribband" (29), "To her againe, she burning in a Feaver" (34 - 35), "Separation of Lovers" (61 - 62), and "To the Painter" (106 - 107).

8. Selig, on p. 67, and throughout, talks of Carew's use of hair as an emblem and of the power with which he endows it to bind souls for eternity.

9. Cf. Selig, pp. 30 ff., where he also has an interesting discussion of Carew's fondness for such images as "admantine" and "pearlie."

10. See Schoff, p. 14, on the power of the lady's beauty to attract even insects.

11. Schoff, p. 14, calls this "the most perfect thing of its kind in English verse." Good discussions appear in Blanshard, pp. 216 - 17, and in Selig, p. 22.

12. A discussion of the genre is given in Kitty W. Scoular, *Natural Magic: Studies in the Presentation of Nature in English Poetry from Spenser to Marvell* (Oxford, 1965), pp. 100 - 102.

13. For the popularity of this theme, see Scoular, p. 66.

14. W. J. Courthope, *A History of English Poetry* (London, 1903), III, 244 - 45. Dunlap cites a parallel in Donne's "Elegie VIII" (p. 270), and Blanshard defends the image (p. 215).

15. Cf. Miner, p. 135.

16. Among the other poems using alchemical images, see "Upon the Kings sicknesse" (35 - 36), "A Rapture" (49 - 53), "To the Countesse of Anglesie" (69 - 71), the Donne elegy (71 - 74), "In answer of an Elegiacall Letter" (74 - 77), and "To the Queene" (90 - 91).

17. Dunlap, p. 231, offers the possibility that a real house with animal statuary is intended.

18. For other Carew treatments of love's entry, see "To a Lady not yet enjoy'd by her Husband" (36) and "Separation of Lovers" (61 - 62).

19. Selig has an informative discussion of this poem, pp. 24 - 26; see also p. 128, n.

20. Dunlap, p. 232, points out that the heading of the poem as set by Lawes only makes the identity of Celia more uncertain.

21. See Selig, pp. 74 - 80.

22. Carl Holliday, *The Cavalier Poets: Their Lives, Their Day, and Their Poetry* (New York and Washington, 1911), p. 84, finds this conceit, though controlled by reason, "bad enough."

23. See Blanshard, pp. 222 - 23; cf. Selig, p. 48.

24. The poem is reminiscent of Donne's "The Extasie." Selig, p. 69, uses it to contrast Carew and Donne.

25. Perhaps this is an example of one of the few passages in Carew's poetry that are not well thought out.

26. George Saintsbury, *A History of Elizabethan Literature* (London, 1887), p. 361. See also Blanshard, "Thomas Carew and the Cavalier Poets," *Transactions of the Wisconsin Academy of Sciences, Arts and Letters,* 43 (1954), 98; Maurice Hussey, ed., *Jonson and the Cavaliers* (New York, 1964), p. 153; Richmond, p. 79; and Louis Untermeyer, *Lives of the Poets* (New York, 1959), p. 164.

27. Joseph H. Summers, *The Heirs of Donne and Jonson* (New York and London, 1970), p. 69.

28. For the flower symbolism, see Selig, p. 87.

29. Cf. Schoff, pp. 11 and 23 - 24, n.

30. See Miner, p. 255.

31. E.g., Selig, p. 68.

32. See Schoff, p. 11; Selig, p. 20. The term "sonnet" was used very loosely in Carew's period.

33. See Selig, pp. 126 - 28. Louis L. Martz, ed., *The Anchor Anthology of Seventeenth Century Verse* (Garden City, New York, 1969), I, xxi - xxii, finds it "Metaphysical."

34. E.g., "Jealousie" (59 - 60), "Incommunicabilitie of Love" (62), "A Lover in the disguise of an Amazon" (63), the epilogue to a play (127 - 28), "Mediocritie in love rejected" (12 - 13), and "To my Mistris, I burning in love" (34).

35. See F. R. Leavis, *Revaluation: Tradition and Development in English Poetry* (London, 1936), pp. 16, 27.

36. On the sources, see Dunlap, p. 221; Richmond, p. 205; Dalglish, p. 153; B. King, "The Strategy of Carew's Wit," *A Review of English Literature,* 5 (1964), 43; Blanshard, "Thomas Carew and the Cavalier Poets," p. 98.

37. Dalglish, p. 152, see this as a "fine example of Carew's sense of structure." See also Saintsbury, p. 362, and Sembower, p. 458.

38. See Selig, pp. 64 ff., and King, pp. 45 - 46.

39. Not exclusively Donnean, of course. Cf. Schoff, p. 15.

40. Cf. Richmond, p. 140.

41. See Dunlap, p. 222, and Edward Bliss Reed, *English Lyrical Poetry from Its Origins to the Present Time* (New Haven, 1912), p. 251.

42. On the last stanza, see R. E., "Carew's 'Disdaine Returned,' " *Explicator,* 11 (1953), Q3; Macdonald Emslie, "Carew's 'Disdaine Returned,' " *Explicator,* 12 (1953), Item 4; Donald C. Baker, "Carew's

'Disdaine Returned,' " *Explicator,* 11 (1953), Item 54.

43. Dunlap, p. xxxi, thinks it probably refers to Carew's sojourn in France with Sir Edward Herbert.

44. For an informative discussion, see Selig, pp. 106 - 107.

Chapter Three

1. P. 18: "Such nonsense, which ranks beside the worst in Crashaw, is inexcusable because it is irresponsible. The obscurity of the stanza assures its failure as intended compliment, and also as poetry. We must reject it because it has neither an imaginative nor an intellectual focus. The trouble with this kind of writing is not that the poet takes great pains to elaborate the petty . . . but that he does not take enough pains to turn his material to poetic account." Blanshard, in "Thomas Carew's Master Figures," pp. 218 - 19, discusses the poem's use of the rhetorical figure of *expeditio.*

2. Felix E. Schelling, *A Book of Seventeenth Century Lyrics* (Boston, 1899), pp. xii - xiii, uses this poem to show Carew's hyperbole.

3. See Selig, p. 98.

4. Robin Skelton, *Cavalier Poets* (London, 1960), p. 18, finds the perception not extraordinary but "absolutely faithful to the psychology of the male animal."

5. Untermeyer, p. 164.

6. Martz, p. xxi.

7. The first two stanzas of this poem and of "A Looking-Glasse" (19) are virtually identical. In the latter, however, the lady is warned not to look (1) lest she kill herself as she kills him and others with her "killing eye" and (2) lest she fall in love with her own image. Her true glass is the speaker, whose paleness from unrequited love truthfully reveals her "faire face" but "cruell minde." In "On his Mistress lookeinge in a glasse," his tears become her true mirror, and she "cannot know/How faire [a pun?] you are, but by my woe." See also "To A. D. unreasonable distrustfull of her owne beauty" (84 - 86) and "On sight of a Gentlewomans face in the water" (102).

8. Pp. 81 - 82.

9. The image of the "quiet Eddie" is used in "To the Countesse of Anglesie upon the immoderatly-by-her-lamented death of her Husband" (69 - 71) to summarize the life of the deceased. Schelling, p. xxxv, n., finds lines 59 - 68 part of the portrait of Carew's ideal man.

10. C. V. Wedgwood, *Poetry and Politics Under the Stuarts* (Cambridge, England, 1960), p. 192, quotes the political ballad.

11. Like so many seventeenth-century poets, Carew seems to have been fond of using images from the Song of Solomon; other examples include "A Pastorall Dialogue" (45 - 46) and "On a Damaske rose sticking upon a Ladies breast" (108).

12. P. 13.

13. Dunlap, p. 268, suggests Joannes Bonefonius as a source.

14. "For a Picture where a Queen Laments over the Tombe of a slaine Knight" (81) deserves mention here, though not in the precise genre of "To the Painter." While a weak performance, it does show further influence of Continental poets, especially Marino.

15. Selig has a good discussion of the poem on pp. 121 - 25 and reports: ". . . there is no better example than this poem of Carew's ability to infuse new life into tired clichés" (p. 121).

16. Selig, p. 19. Ironically, Carew, as Paulina Palmer, "Thomas Carew: An Allusion to 'Venus and Adonis,'" *N&Q*, 13 (1966), 255 - 56, points out, is using Shakespeare here and elsewhere in the poem.

17. Selig, p. 52, uses this poem to distinguish the "two voices" in Carew's poems.

18. Dunlap, pp. liii - liv, and Selig, pp. 102 - 104, use this poem to contrast Carew and Donne.

19. On the differences between Carew and Donne, see Selig, p. 16, and Joan Bennett, *Five Metaphysical Poets* (Cambridge, England, 1964), p. 134.

20 See D. F. Rauber, "Carew Redivivus," *TSLL*, 13 (1971), 25 - 26. For other poems treating "means and extremes," see Chapter 2, n. 34.

21. Sembower, pp. 457 - 58.

22. See Chapter 2, n. 34, and Chapter 3, n. 20.

23. Dunlap, p. 271, calls it a "grave little essay" and hypothesizes that it "may represent youthful work suggested by Sir Thomas Overbury's *A Wife* (1614) and the several imitations which followed it."

24. Another curious love composition is "A Pastorall Dialogue" (45 - 46), interesting for its echoes of *A Midsummer Night's Dream* and *Romeo and Juliet* and for its frame. The speakers are a shepherd, a nymph, and the Chorus. An intensification of the distancing natural to pastoral is gained by having the nymph and shepherd relate the parting between another pastoral couple, who try to but cannot "pinion *Time*, and chase / The day for ever from this place" (ll. 29 - 30). The effect is similar to that of Shakespeare having Romeo and Juliet part through the mechanism of a parodic aubade.

Chapter Four

1. King, pp. 47 - 48, has a good discussion of the attempt to gain equality.

2. E.g., Dunlap, p. 254; George Williamson, *The Donne Tradition. A Study in English Poetry from Donne to the Death of Cowley* (New York, 1930), p. 204; and Untermeyer, p. 164.

3. Herbert J. C. Grierson, ed., *The Poems of John Donne* (London, 1912), I, 15, 245.

4. Ll. 13 - 24 were set to music by Henry Lawes. Selig, pp. 62 - 67, uses

the "poem-within-the-poem" as an example of the "Golden" poetry of the Age of Elizabeth and provides an extended discussion of it.

5. Much of the imagery of this poem recurs with some frequency in Carew's works; e.g., spices, "disheveld tresses," pearls, the halcyon.

6. For good discussions, see Blanshard, "Thomas Carew's Master Figures," p. 224, and Schoff, p. 13.

7. P. 74.

8. Cf. "To Will. Davenant my Friend" (98), l. 18: "barren and insipid Truth. . . ."

9. On the difficulty of identifying this allusion, see Paulina Palmer, "Thomas Carew's Reference to 'The Shepherd's Paradise,'" *N&Q*, 13 (1966), 303 - 304.

10. Wedgwood, p. 44.

11. Williamson, *Seventeenth Century Contexts* (Chicago, 1969), p. 123, maintains that Carew describes the "strong-lined" school in ll. 37 - 39.

12. Summers points out that, "As with Donne's *First Anniversary*, the very brilliance of the poem makes paradoxical its central thesis that the glory has all departed" (p. 65).

13. Selig, p. 170.

14. Of ll. 25 - 53, Summers remarks: "Those marvellously energetic run-over couplets, the quick and imaginative changes of both rhythms and images, the imitation of rough and masterful masculinity are evidence of Donne's still-living poetic genius" (p. 65). Hussey calls the elegy "a re-enactment of the style of Donne that Carew did not repeat" (p. 153).

15. Selig, pp. 156 - 57, has a good discussion of the colloquial idiom of this poem.

16. A. J. Smith, "The Failure of Love: Love Lyrics after Donne," *Stratford-Upon-Avon Studies*, 11 (1970), 53, finds that "Carew gives the game away when he resolves the argument for singleness of love with the image of a wolf which starves because it can't decide between two sheep before it. . . . Yet if all these poems assume a motive of predatory appetite they are chiefly conscious of how society must inhibit its scope, and much of the poet's art goes in refining erotic provocation, or throwing a glittering veil over the raw impulse. . . ."

17. See, for example, "To A. L. Perswasions to love" (4 - 6), "A Ladies prayer to Cupid" (131), and "In the person of a Lady to her inconstant servant" (40).

18. For additional information, see Michel Grivelet, " 'Th' Untun'd Kennell': Note sur Thomas Heywood et le Théâtre sous Charles 1er," *Études Anglaises*, 7 (1954), 101 - 106.

19. Cf. "Obsequies to the Lady Anne Hay" (67 - 68), ll. 45 - 46.

Chapter Five

1. Rauber, pp. 22 - 23, suggests that "Surely it ['To A. L.'] is one of the most complex *carpe diem* poems in the literature, comparing very favorably with Marvell's 'To His Coy Mistress.' "

2. Pp. 361 - 62.

3. For differences between Samuel Daniel's and Carew's treatment of Marino, see Dunlap, pp. lv - lvi. For a contrast between Carew and both Donne and Jonson, see Rauber, pp. 20 - 23.

4. Miner, p. 106.

5. Cf. Smith, p. 53: ". . . Henrietta Maria queens it over a Court of Love. The new style of court hyperbole defines the queen's relationship to the king in erotic terms, extolling her power to control and make stable the wild lusts of masculine nature; and the new version of order, as of chivalry, turns on the natural capacity of the right female to hold a man to herself, so centring his errant fancies and concentrating his powers. . . ."

6. This is reminiscent of Donne in "The Canonization," ll. 19 - 27, where he draws on the alchemical hermaphrodite.

7. "Upon Master W. Mountague his returne from travell" (77 - 78) is discussed in Chapter 4.

8. This is the term used by Geoffrey Walton, *Metaphysical to Augustan. Studies in Tone and Sensibility in the Seventeenth Century* (London, 1955), pp. 34 - 35.

9. Hussey, p. 152, considers the conceit on self-sacrifice to be "almost . . . Metaphysical."

10. Schoff, pp. 17 - 18, provides an excellent analysis of these lines. The passage anticipates *Coelum Britannicum.*

11. Alastair Fowler, *Triumphal Forms: Structural Patterns in Elizabethan Poetry* (Cambridge, England, 1970), pp. 156 - 57, has an unusual and interesting reading of what Carew is taking off from for this poem.

12. Another epithalamion, not addressed to any particular persons, is "An Hymeneall Dialogue" (66), interesting for the fact that the bride as well as the groom preaches the doctrine of the "mutuall change / Of soules" and for the image of her making a "nest" in the bosom of the groom.

13. See also the discussion in Chapter 4.

14. As several critics have suggested, if the "royall Goth" of the sixth stanza is Gustavus Adolphus, the poem must have been written before his death on November 6, 1632.

15. It was Elsie Duncan-Jones, in "Carew's 'Upon the Kings Sicknesse,'" *Explicator*, 13 (1954), Item 19, who first pointed out that l. 18 refers not to the King, but to his subjects.

16. Blanshard, "Carew and Jonson," *SP*, 52 (1955), 195 - 211, believes that Jonson's epitaphs are responsible for the three on Mary Villiers and at least for the form of the one on Maria Wentworth.

17. *Select Beauties of Ancient English Poetry* (London, 1787), II, 154.

18. "Thomas Carew and the Cavalier Poets," p. 101.

19. "Note A," pp. 37 - 38. For others on the combined influences, see Dalglish, p. 151; Margaret Willy, ed., *The Metaphysical Poets* (Columbia, S. C., 1971), p. 48; and Selig, pp. 112 - 14.

20. Summers, p. 70, suggests that it is "indecorous." But Margaret Willy, p. 48, considers it a "brilliant conceit," "a flash of metaphysical wit at its most epigrammatically effective, by which in a sense the somewhat conventionally unremarkable sentiments of the whole epitaph are themselves 'justifi'd.' " Schoff says, p. 20: "It is . . . an audacious conceit, and I know of nothing in Donne or Marvell which is at once more startling and farreaching in its implications, and more consummately tactful and decorous in its treatment."

Chapter Six

1. See Dunlap, p. 273.

2. Cited in Dunlap, p. 273.

3. Dunlap suggests, p. 274, that the masque performed before the Earl of Arundel in Germany was not Carew's.

4. Milton does seem to be aware of it in "On the Morning of Christ's Nativity," l. 68. Yet Carew sees the doubleness of the Medusa image, for Government has the symbol of the head on his shield. Cf. Mercury on Poenia, l. 651.

5. Momus alludes to Shrove Tuesday in ll. 128 - 29.

6. Smith, pp. 53 - 54.

7. *Lectures on the Comic Writers, The Complete Works of William Hazlitt*, ed. P. P. Howe (New York, 1967), VI, 54 - 55.

8. P. 22.

9. E. E. Duncan-Jones, "Carew and Guez de Balzac," *MLR*, 46, (1951), 439 - 40, made the identification of Balzac.

10. Blanshard, "Carew and Jonson," records this special indebtedness.

11. A more political reason, directly from Bruno, is given in ll. 230 - 33: ". . . *Jove* is growne old and fearefull, apprehends a subversion of his Empire, and doubts lest Fate should introduce a legall succession in the legitimate heire, by repossessing the Titanian line, and hence springs all this innovation."

12. Dunlap, p. 278, records recent reformations.

13. P. 20.

14. Summers, p. 75, interprets Hedone's rejection as an admission by Carew: "It suggests . . . that Carew, like some later poets, had come to know by experience that a simple sensuous hedonism may be one of the most painful of all creeds, particularly for a man past thirty-five, but that it was about all he had. . . ."

15. Lawes was apparently connected with both Carew's and Milton's masques, as were Lord Brackley and Mr. Thomas Egerton, sons of the Earl of Bridgewater, who played in both, their roles much greater, of course, in the Ludlow production.

16. Cited in Dunlap, p. 273.

Chapter Seven

1. James E. Ruoff, "Thomas Carew's Early Reputation," *N&Q*, 4 (1957), 61 - 62.

2. *The Great Assises* is discussed in Dunlap, pp. xlvii - xlix. The documents for assessing Carew's early reputation have been exhaustively studied by Dunlap, pp. xlvi - li, and especially by Arthur H. Nethercot, in three articles: "The Reputation of the 'Metaphysical Poets' during the Seventeenth Century," *JEGP*, 23 (1924), 173 - 98; "The Reputation of the 'Metaphysical Poets' during the Age of Pope," *PQ*, 4 (1925), 161 - 79; "The Reputation of the 'Metaphysical Poets' during the Age of Johnson and the 'Romantic Revival,' " *SP*, 22 (1925), 81 - 132.

3. Cited in Dunlap, p. xlvi.

4. The poems addressed to Carew, including Townshend's, are reprinted in Dunlap, pp. 207 - 10, along with the two letters from Suckling and Carew's answers, pp. 211 - 13.

5. James A. Means, "An Echo of Carew in Robert Blair," *AN&Q*, 7 (1969), 86.

6. J. C. Maxwell, "Lucy Ashton's Song," *N&Q*, 195 (1950), 210.

7. The later editions are described in Dunlap, pp. lxxvi - lxxviii, the most important being those of W. Carew Hazlitt (the first scholarly edition, 1870), Joseph Woodfall Ebsworth (1893), Arthur Vincent (1899), and R. G. Howarth (1931, containing only the poems, along with those of Suckling, Lovelace, and Lord Herbert of Cherbury—i.e., *Minor Poets of the Seventeenth Century*).

8. For the musical settings, see Dunlap, pp. 289 - 93; for the miscellanies in which the poems appeared, pp. xlix - l.

9. P. 177.

10. These are considered in detail by Nethercot, "The Reputation of the 'Metaphysical Poets' during the Age of Johnson and the 'Romantic Revival.' "

11. *Ibid.*, p. 108.

12. I, xl.

13. Howe, VI, 311 - 12.

14. P. 116.

15. P. 177.

16. Hardin Craig, *The Literature of the English Renaissance, 1485 - 1660* (New York, 1962), p. 208.

Selected Bibliography

PRIMARY SOURCES

DUNLAP, RHODES, ed. *The Poems of Thomas Carew with His Masque Coelum Britannicum*. London: Oxford University Press, 1949; rpt. 1970.

EBSWORTH, JOSEPH WOODFALL, ed. *The Poems and Masque of Thomas Carew*. London: Reeves and Turner, 1893.

HAZLITT, W. CAREW, ed. *The Poems of Thomas Carew*. London: The Roxburghe Library, 1870.

HOWARTH, R. G., ed. *Minor Poets of the Seventeenth Century*. London: Dent (Everyman's Library), 1931.

VINCENT, ARTHUR, ed. *The Poems of Thomas Carew*. London: Lawrence & Bullen, Ltd.; New York: Charles Scribner's Sons, 1899.

WALKLEY, THOMAS, ed. *The Workes of Thomas Carew Esquire*. London: I.D., 1640, 1642, 1651.

SECONDARY SOURCES

BAKER, DONALD C. "Carew's 'Disdaine Returned.'" *Explicator*, 11 (1953), Item 54. On the last two lines.

BIGGS, ALAN J. "Carew and Shakespeare." *Notes and Queries*, 3 (1956), 225. On "To her in absence. A Ship."

BLANSHARD, RUFUS A. "Carew and Jonson." *Studies in Philology*, 52 (1955), 195 - 211. A close analysis of Carew's (unacknowledged) debt to Jonson.

————. "Thomas Carew and the Cavalier Poets." *Transactions of the Wisconsin Academy of Sciences, Arts and Letters*, 43 (1954), 97 - 105. Contrasts Carew with the Cavaliers to reveal his individuality.

————. "Thomas Carew's Master Figures." *Boston University Studies in English*, 3 (1957), 214 - 27. Carew's use of four figures from George Puttenham's *The Arte of English Poesie*.

BUSH, DOUGLAS. *English Literature in the Earlier Seventeenth Century, 1600 - 1660*. New York: Oxford University Press, 1962, 2nd edition. A brief, general view of Carew, pp. 119 - 21.

CRAIG, HARDIN. *The Literature of the English Renaissance, 1485 - 1660*. London: Oxford University Press, 1950; rpt. New York: Collier Books, 1962. Brief mention of Carew as a "typical" poet.

DALGLISH, JACK. *Eight Metaphysical Poets*. London: Heinemann, 1961. Brief but good account of Carew, the leading representative of the Caroline school.

DUNCAN-JONES, E[LSIE] E. "Carew and Guez de Balzac." *Modern Language Review*, 46 (1951), 439 - 40. Identifies Balzac in *Coelum Britannicum*.

————. "Carew's 'Upon the Kings Sicknesse.' " *Explicator*, 13 (1954), Item 19. Disagrees with Dunlap on l. 18.

DUNLAP, RHODES. "Thomas Carew, Thomas Carey, and 'The Sovereign of the Seas.' " *Modern Language Notes*, 56 (1941), 268 - 71. Not by the poet.

E., R. "Carew's 'Disdain Returned.' " *Explicator*, 11 (1953), Q3. Requests an explanation of the last two lines.

EMSLIE, MACDONALD. "Carew's 'Disdaine Returned.' " *Explicator*, 12 (1953), Item 4. On the end couplet.

FOWLER, ALASTAIR. *Triumphal Forms: Structural Patterns in Elizabethan Poetry*. Cambridge: Cambridge University Press, 1970. "An Hymeneall Song on the Nuptials of the lady *Ann Wentworth*, and the Lord *Lovelace*" mimes the divisions of the year and the wedding night.

GRIERSON, HERBERT J. C., ed. *Metaphysical Lyrics and Poems of the Seventeenth Century. Donne to Butler*. London: Oxford University Press, 1921; rpt. Galaxy, 1959. Dated but essential. Carew best reflects Charles's court. Focused attention on his classification.

HAZLITT, WILLIAM. *The Complete Works of William Hazlitt*. Ed. P. P. Howe. 21 vols. New York: AMS Press, Inc., 1967 [1931]. Influential and generally denigrating comments (Carew an "elegant court-trifler").

HEADLEY, HENRY. *Select Beauties of Ancient English Poetry*. 2 vols. London: T. Cadell, 1787. Good on the relation between Carew and Waller.

HOLLIDAY, CARL. *The Cavalier Poets: Their Lives, Their Day, and Their Poetry*. New York and Washington: The Neale Publishing Company, 1911. Some biographical errors but still worth seeing. Carew points the way to Neoclassicism.

HOWARTH, R. G. "A Poem by Carew?" *Notes and Queries*, 197 (1952), 518. "The Departure" is probably by Thomas Carey.

HUSSEY, MAURICE, ed. *Jonson and the Cavaliers*. New York: Barnes and Noble, Inc., 1964. Short but worthwhile treatment of Carew with good notes on six poems.

JOHNSON, PAULA. "Carew's 'A Rapture': The Dynamics of Fantasy." *Studies in English Literature, 16* (1976), 145 - 55. The poem distinguishes what is, what may be postulated as fiction, and what can never be.

KING, B[RUCE]. "The Strategy of Carew's Wit." *AReview of English Literature*, 5 (1964), 42 - 51. Carew's wit imposes order on the chaos of man's inner realities.

LEAVIS, F. R. *Revaluation: Tradition and Development in English Poetry*. London: Chatto and Windus, 1936; rpt. 1959. Essential reading. Places Carew in the "line of wit": from Jonson (and Donne) through Carew and Marvell to Pope.

MARTZ, LOUIS L., ed. *The Anchor Anthology of Seventeenth Century Verse*. Garden City, New York: Doubleday and Co., Inc., 1969. Vol. I, rev. ed. of *The Meditative Poem* (1963). Illustrates the Metaphysical style with "To my inconstant Mistris."

MAXWELL, J. C. "Lucy Ashton's Song." *Notes and Queries*, 195 (1950), 210. Scott's echoes of Carew.

MEANS, JAMES A. "An Echo of Carew in Robert Blair." *American Notes and Queries*, 7 (1969), 86. The use by Blair of a line from the Donne elegy.

MINER, EARL. *The Cavalier Mode from Jonson to Cotton.* Princeton: Princeton University Press, 1971. Essential background. Disagrees with Leavis on Carew and the "line of wit."

NETHERCOT, ARTHUR H. "The Reputation of the 'Metaphysical Poets' during the Seventeenth Century." *Journal of English and Germanic Philology*, 23 (1924), 173 - 98. Slow decline in reputation as a result of changing conceptions of style and wit.

————. "The Reputation of the 'Metaphysical Poets' during the Age of Pope." *Philological Quarterly*, 4 (1925), 161 - 79. Carew maintained a minor place as a courtier, the writer of a masque, and a poet of lightness and grace. His extravagancies were noted.

————. "The Reputation of the 'Metaphysical Poets' during the Age of Johnson and the 'Romantic Revival.'" *Studies in Philology*, 22 (1925), 81 - 132. The eighteenth century preferred the smoothness of Waller. The Romantics liked Carew's grace.

PALMER, PAULINA. "Thomas Carew: An Allusion to 'Venus and Adonis.'" *Notes and Queries*, 13 (1966), 255 - 56. Carew uses Shakespeare in "A Pastorall Dialogue" (45) and "A Song" (105).

————. "Thomas Carew's Reference to 'The Shepherd's Paradise.'" *Notes and Queries*, 13 (1966), 303 - 304. The reference in *Coelum Britannicum* is to a pastoral play by Montagu.

POWELL, C. L. "New Material on Thomas Carew." *Modern Language Review*, 11 (1916), 285 - 97. Updated by Dunlap but containing interesting observations on some of the poems.

QUILLER-COUCH, SIR ARTHUR. *Adventures in Criticism.* Cambridge: Cambridge University Press, 1926 [1896]. An amusing discourse on the pronunciation of Carew's name.

RAUBER, D. F. "Carew Redivivus." *Texas Studies in Language and Literature*, 13 (1971), 17 - 28. Essential. Sees Carew as the most intellectual poet of his period.

REED, EDWARD BLISS. *English Lyrical Poetry from Its Origins to the Present Time.* New Haven: Yale University Press, 1912. Good discussion of individual poems. Carew shows change in lyric poem to a graceful compliment.

RICHMOND, H. M. *The School of Love: The Evolution of the Stuart Love Lyric.* Princeton: Princeton University Press, 1964. Good discussions of several individual poems, especially "Ingratefull beauty threatned."

RUOFF, JAMES E. "Thomas Carew's Early Reputation." *Notes and Queries*, 4 (1957), 61 - 62. Carew's poems disparaged in the House of Commons.

SAINTSBURY, GEORGE. *A History of Elizabethan Literature.* New York: Russell and Russell, 1970 [1887]. Provides a life of Carew and high praise.

SCHELLING, FELIX E[MMANUEL], ed. *A Book of Seventeenth Century Lyrics.* Boston: Ginn and Co., 1899. Good notes on individual poems. Carew (and Herrick) typical of the secular seventeenth-century lyric at its best.

SCHOFF, FRANCIS G. "Thomas Carew: Son of Ben or Son of Spenser?" *Discourse,* 1 (1958), 8 - 24. Invaluable article pressing for recognition of Elizabethan influences on Carew.

SCOULAR, KITTY W. *Natural Magic: Studies in the Presentation of Nature in English Poetry from Spenser to Marvell.* Oxford: Clarendon Press, 1965. Provides background for the poetry of "small creatures."

SELIG, EDWARD I. *The Flourishing Wreath: A Study of Thomas Carew's Poetry.* New Haven: Yale University Press, 1958; rept. Hamden, Connecticut: Archon Books, 1970. Heretofore the only book-length study of Carew. Examines his genres and his relation to music.

SEMBOWER, CHARLES J. "A Note on the Verse Structure of Carew," *Studies in Language and Literature in Celebration of the Seventieth Birthday of James Morgan Hart.* New York: Henry Holt and Co., 1910, pp. 456 - 66. Carew's variety seldom organic. Best at the "arch pretense of logic."

SHAPIRO, I. A. "Carew's 'Obsequies to the Lady Anne Hay.' " *Notes and Queries,* 196 (1951), 7 - 8. Probably written to ingratiate Carew with the Earl and Countess of Carlisle.

SKELTON, ROBIN. *Cavalier Poets.* London: Longmans, Green, and Co., 1960. Carew a master in the true Cavalier tone: careless ease, humor, and subtle inflections of the voice.

SMITH, A. J. "The Failure of Love: Love Lyrics after Donne." *Stratford-Upon-Avon Studies,* 11 (1970), 41 - 71. Good on several individual poems. Carew (with Suckling and Rochester) marks a shift in attitudes to love from 1600 to 1700.

SUMMERS, JOSEPH H. *The Heirs of Donne and Jonson.* New York and London: Oxford University Press, 1970. Good, especially on individual poems. Did care about poetry. Knowledge and mastery of Donne and Jonson surpass that of any other poet up to 1640.

SYLVESTER, R[ICHARD] S., ed. *The Anchor Anthology of Seventeenth-Century Verse.* Garden City, New York: Doubleday and Co., Inc., 1969. Vol. II. Good background and notes on poems. Carew a Cavalier drawing on Jonson, Donne, and the Petrarchans.

UNTERMEYER, LOUIS. *Lives of the Poets: The Story of One Thousand Years of English and American Poetry.* New York: Simon and Schuster, 1959. Brief but acute comments. A dozen or so of the short poems among the best of the period.

WEDGWOOD, C. V. *Poetry and Politics Under the Stuarts.* Cambridge: Cambridge University Press, 1960. Good as background. Examines Carew's involvement with the court.

WILLIAMSON, GEORGE. *The Donne Tradition. A Study in English Poetry from Donne to the Death of Cowley.* New York: The Noonday Press, 1958 [1930]. Places Carew on the "fringe" of the Donne tradition.

Index

DATE DUE
